# *Natural Helping Networks*

# Natural Helping Networks

## A Strategy for Prevention

ALICE H. COLLINS &
DIANE L. PANCOAST

National Association of Social Workers

1425 H Street, N.W. Washington, D.C. 20005

*International Standard Book No.: 0–87101–070–4*
*Library of Congress Catalog Card No.: 76–10027*
*NASW Publication No.: CBC–070–C*
*Printed in U.S.A.*

# Contents

# Introduction

Almost ten years ago, in the course of a demonstration research project on a new kind of family day care service, we made an unexpected discovery that seemed to us to have great potential for the success of our current undertaking and for social work practice in general. We had intended to initiate an information and referral exchange for family day care givers and users. But when we investigated our target neighborhood, we found that there already were small neighborhood networks through which many service needs were met informally and naturally. The individuals involved in them took them so much for granted that they hardly recognized them for what they were. The networks seemed to revolve around and be facilitated by certain central figures who saw themselves and were seen by others as willing to invest themselves in helping to make arrangements, in giving advice, and in providing direct help. Our major interest was in the family day care networks, but we soon saw that these networks provided other kinds of help and were themselves part of a web of neighborhood service networks. We modified our procedures to center on what we came to call natural neighbors in natural family day care networks that were already functioning well. We tried both to learn all we could about them and also to develop and test ways in which we as social workers could relate to them, support their current operations, and encourage them to broaden their scope in the future.

We had come across this phenomenon of neighborhood networks while analyzing the results of a survey of family day care givers in the target neighborhood. The survey had been undertaken originally because, to our surprise, a review of the literature on child care and working mothers had yielded us virtually no data about family day care givers: what they liked and disliked about giving care, how arrangements were made, and what would attract them to join the information and referral exchange we had in mind. Without this information, we believed that the exchange—the innovative child care service we were funded to demonstrate—would have little hope of recruiting women who would be excellent day care givers after we had trained them and established contacts between them and the neighborhood's working mothers of all socioeconomic levels.

The survey had lived up to a well-known definition of research: a process that takes longer, tells less, and costs more than anticipated! Although census statistics and professional opinions indicated that the neighborhood to be surveyed had a large number of family day care givers from which a sample of 100 might well be drawn, it was only after great effort that we emerged with a universe of 27 women who admitted to being family day care givers and who would agree to an interview. To make the greatest possible use of these meager data, we ranked the respondents according to characteristics of performance and personality that are widely accepted as essential to good child care. Here we made our first discovery: the highest ranked individuals had several other characteristics in common. They were much less mobile than other residents of the area; they were in the 30- to 45-year age range; they had intact families and children of school age or under in the home; they appeared to have a mature interest in other people, both children and adults. Common characteristics were not found with respect to their educational levels, which ranged from completion of eighth grade to graduation from college. Nor were they evident in their economic situations, which ranged from subsistence income to over $15,000 a year.

Predictably, our visibility in the neighborhood while conducting the survey led to requests for help in finding day care. Although a formal service was still to be organized, we felt some obligation to respond as best we could to such requests and did so by asking some of the top-ranked day care givers whether they could take on another child. They were not surprised to be asked and often replied that, although they could not give care, they would contact a neighbor or friend and would help make the arrangements. We began to see that there was already a flourishing network for making informal day care arrangements and that certain central figures in the network acted voluntarily as advisers and matchmakers, matching persons who needed services with persons who could provide them. We began to wonder about the accuracy of the often repeated assertion that good family day care was in short supply.[1] There were certainly many changes in arrangements but these might have more to do with the kinds of families involved in the transactions than with the lack of available care givers. Families having young children made the arrangements and in doing so had to cope with such varied problems as schedules and turnover of employment for both sets of parents, pregnancy, divorce, and the many adjustments necessary for compatibility when two families care for the same child.

As we worked with the survey data, we were also learning more by personal observation and by word of mouth from neighbors and professional colleagues about some of the individuals we had interviewed and ranked. To our chagrin, we found that two whom we had rated as satisfactory proved neglectful and unreliable. The closer we came to the organization of the exchange, the more we questioned its chances of success. We asked ourselves how we would be able to avoid misjudgments in making the necessary multitudinous arrangements, knowing that the size of our staff would be stringently limited to make the service economical and therefore feasible when applied on a national scale. How would we know from our central office—although her neighbors knew it well—that Mrs. Brown, whose house and fenced yard and pleasant cooperation had earned her a place as a day care giver on the exchange, also held a swing-shift job and left her 13-year-old daughter to take charge of the four children in her care? And how would we go about recruiting the constant supply of good day care givers who, as we now recognized, would be required? How would we find good prospects behind all those neighborhood doors that had failed to open for our survey? How find them among women whose excellence as day care givers seemed to be in direct ratio to their family-centered status?

Perhaps our new discovery about central figures who met neighborhood needs could provide some answers. Once more we turned to the professional literature to see what others had learned about natural networks and their value in service delivery. And once more we found almost no useful references. There were initial reports about projects that recognized how important indigenous individuals were for interpreting their cultures to professionals, and there were many accounts of how such individuals were incorporated into agency staffs as paraprofessionals who could go up a career ladder to full professional status.[2] But this approach did not seem appropriate for working with the networks we were beginning to recognize. The top-ranked women we had interviewed had chosen their home-centered role, liked it, and would not be likely to give it up to become agency employees.

In some descriptive studies by sociologists and anthropologists, we found descriptions of similar natural neighbors—although they were not so designated—and of natural networks.[3] At the same time, we discovered that there were conflicting views in the behavioral sciences about the very existence of neighbors and neighborhoods.

Our review of the literature strongly suggested that the most scientific response to our discovery would be to undertake comprehensive, long-term data collection and analysis to find out whether natural neighbors did exist in natural networks and, if they did, how they functioned. We would then have some basis for planning a method of intervention and justifying it with careful documentation.

Our grant, however, required us to demonstrate a service and evaluate it within a relatively short period of time. Even if this period could have been extended, we would not have chosen to change it. We had some convictions, based on experience and observation of social work surveys of need, that the most dependable data for planning future service delivery could be gathered from the operation of a functioning service rather than from the answers to questions about a projected one. Nevertheless, we wished to avoid the all-too-frequent professional practice of deciding what was needed, supplying it, and evaluating its effectiveness for those who used it—neglecting to consider those who did not use it.

## *AN OFFER TO NATURAL NEIGHBORS*

We decided to combine observation with action, and to gamble that what we had glimpsed was indeed pay dirt. We would try to identify the natural neighbors in a given area and then ask them to help us learn how their family day care networks operated day by day. In exchange, we would offer to be their colleagues in providing the best possible care for children and their families, which we assumed was a mutual objective and which we hoped they would be able to extend throughout their neighborhood.

Although we had many misgivings about how acceptable this somewhat one-sided offer would be, we were confident that we could carry out our consultative role, since we had had considerable experience in consultation with professional caretakers. We believed that the techniques used with these caretakers would work equally well with nonprofessional natural neighbors—a hypothesis that proved to be almost correct.

In fact, the natural neighbors' response both with respect to our learning about their networks and being their colleagues was much quicker and more wholehearted than we had dared hope. They were accustomed to giving information and assistance in their everyday roles and they generously included us. And they were indeed anxious to give the best possible help to those who came to them, not only with problems of family day care but with all kinds of concerns, large and small. They were pleased at being encouraged to reach out beyond their usual circle and involve themselves with neighbors who were strangers, as long as this did not entail any major change in their chosen home-centered role. For our part, we began to realize that natural networks offered possibilities for preventive intervention at every level, and our view of this rich, untapped resource grew constantly wider and more exciting. When our first grant period ended, the Day Care Neighbor Service became a component of the Field Study of the Neighborhood Family Day Care System, and we continued to test and refine our techniques as the window on natural systems opened wider. With the zeal of most discoverers, we talked and wrote about our findings as fast as we made them. By actively soliciting the interest and the ongoing support of other local agencies, we persuaded several of them to undertake experiments with natural networks. For the most part, we found our colleagues interested and even enthusiastic about the concept, but they did not undertake to put it into operation because they were "too busy," or wouldn't know "how to go about it."

We concluded that what was needed was a how-to-do-it publication describing our technique in some detail, as a basis for replication, and we prepared such a handbook.[4] We had several thousand requests for it from all over the country and abroad, and we responded to them with the optimism of evangelists, offering further advice when needed regarding specific interventive efforts. When we made a survey of how ideas set forth in the handbook had been used, we received many agreeable compliments and the disquieting news that almost no one had put our ideas into practice. We turned to the literature on utilization to see what we had done wrong. We found that we were experiencing the normal lag in the adoption of innovative concepts. This finding assuaged the wound to our professional self-esteem. But crises in funding daily reminded us that finding economical and effective means of reaching a large public at the preventive level seemed essential to the survival of the social work profession. And we believed we had found one way to do this.

A positive result of our efforts to stimulate the use of natural networks and to disseminate knowledge about working with them was that we did hear from others, widely scattered geographically, who were having similar experiences with such networks. Their findings, like ours and yet different, showed us new aspects of this resource for service delivery.

At the start of the 1970s, when social work students appeared dissatisfied with traditional approaches and were seeking ways to help bring about social change, it seemed logical to introduce concepts about natural networks to them. Those students to whom the ideas were presented, first in fieldwork placement at a school of social work and then in an elective course, were remarkably quick to understand and make use of them.

We gradually built up a collection of published and unpublished articles pertaining to natural networks that we found stimulating as we tested our theories in practice, revised them, taught them, and observed their application. We believed that if other professionals could have access to our materials, they could compare and contrast the relative effectiveness of various procedures, match specific efforts against their own programs, and perhaps be encouraged to do some exploring and prepare their own publications. This book is one attempt to share what we have learned and to further the exploration of this field.

It can be validly argued that a publication of this kind should properly await definitive research about natural networks and how to work with them. The difficulties inherent in such research are too well known to need further comment, other than to note that in the foreseeable future definitive research can be expected to contribute slowly to the basic services. Meanwhile, the demand for more and better social work services continues to mount, although funds available for providing them do not. It therefore seems permissible to suggest that social workers proceed in their familiar empirical fashion, putting to use what seems practical, testing and reporting on success or failure, and continuously putting new findings into practice and then evaluating the results.

This book is not presented as a final statement of what natural networks are and how they can be used, nor as an exhaustive study of the efforts made to work with them. It is, rather, a compilation of experience that we believe will be as useful to others as it has been to us in clarifying concepts and developing new techniques. We would like to believe that, through our own experience and from the explorations of others, we have uncovered enough about this resource to stimulate other explorers to go further and report what they find, thus providing the profession with ever stronger guidelines for working in an area that holds tremendous promise.

Who "we" denotes requires a word of explanation. The Day Care Exchange proposal was written by Gerald Frey, who was its director for the first year. He was then succeeded by Collins, with Eunice L. Watson as her colleague. The Day Care Neighbor Service was developed and carried forward through their collaboration and with consultation generously given by Dr. Christoph M. Heinicke. When that demonstration was completed, the Day Care Neighbor Service became a component of the Field Study of the Family Day Care System, directed by Arthur C. Emlen, who had already become a part of "us."

Pancoast, who had discovered and worked with a natural network of boarding homes in an urban poverty area independently of the Day Care Neighbor Service, recognized the possibility of introducing social work students to the concept of natural networks and offered both field experience and a course focused in that direction. She became part of "our" discussions, conjectures, arguments, and discoveries as we explored the natural systems.

When finally it seemed time to write down what we had learned, thought, and conjectured, Pancoast and Collins undertook the job, having first consulted with Dr. Gerald Caplan, who had, over the years, greatly influenced all "our" thinking. This book is therefore technically the sole responsibility of its authors, but "we" have all influenced each other to the degree that it is impossible to sort out what is each one's contribution to theory and practice.

Since authors generally do not express their gratitude to themselves for their devotion and support, we will not do so here! On the other hand, we cannot fail to note that without each other, this book would never have been written.

## Notes and References

1. Arthur C. Emlen, "Slogans, Slots, and Slander: The Myth of Day Care Need," *American Journal of Orthopsychiatry*, 43 (January 1973), pp. 23–36.
2. Robert Reiff and Frank Riessman, *The Indigenous Non-professional* (New York: Behavioral Publications, 1965); and Charles Grosser, William E. Henry, and James G. Kelly, eds., *Non-professionals in the Human Services* (San Francisco: Jossey-Bass, 1969).
3. Herbert L. Gans, *The Urban Villagers* (New York: Free Press, 1962); Hylan Lewis, "The Changing Negro Family," in Eli Ginzberg, ed., *The Nation's Children* (New York: Columbia University Press, 1960); and Elizabeth Bott, *Family and Social Network* (2nd ed.; London: Tavistock Publications, 1971).
4. Alice H. Collins and Eunice L. Watson, *The Day Care Neighbor Service: A Handbook for the Organization and Operation of a New Approach to Family Day Care* (Portland, Ore.: Tri-County Community Council, 1969).

# part one

# Natural Networks

# 1

# *Overview of Natural Helping Networks*

The term *network* most accurately describes the relationships that will be the focus of this book. Although much work is currently in progress on networks, the idea of considering a network as an analytical tool rather than as a loose metaphor has developed only recently. This idea is not widely understood in this country and is confined chiefly to anthropology—a discipline whose writings are not generally familiar to social workers.

Craven and Wellman describe the study of networks as an analytical approach to the study of social phenomena.[1] They see it as fundamentally different from the better-developed approach of categorizing individuals and social units according to such constructs as class, role, and institution—but an approach that is equally useful. Network analysis focuses on the links between units rather than on the nature of the units themselves.

The connections between elements of society have long been recognized and have been variously described as webs, networks, the social fabric, action sets, primary and secondary groups, social circles or cliques, systems, and so on. But the study of the interconnections as actual rather than as potential or metaphorical phenomena is rather recent. The development of network analysis can be traced from the exploratory work of three English anthropologists: J. A. Barnes, Elizabeth Bott, and J. Clyde Mitchell, who participated in a seminar with Max Gluckman at the University of Manchester in the early 1950s. Barnes first used the term to describe the relationships of kinship and friendship in a Norwegian fishing village. His original definition of a network is still the most basic one: "a set of points which are joined by lines; the points of the image are people or sometimes groups and the lines indicate which people interact with each other." [2]

Networks, then, consist of people and relationships. Bott used the concept of social networks in her study of working-class London families.[3] Her discovery that the networks of a marital couple affect the nature of their relationship with each other added an important dimension to the concept. This dimension is incorporated in Mitchell's definition of a network as "a specific set of linkages among a defined set of persons, with the . . . property that the characteristics of these linkages as a whole may be used to interpret the social behavior of the persons involved." [4]

We think that, in its practical applicability for social workers, the concept of network has distinct advantages over other ways of describing social collectivities. Social workers are encouraged to consider the person in his setting and to recognize that behavior is a function of both the person and the environment. However, setting and environment are vague concepts and necessarily have unique elements for each individual, so that it is difficult to describe general procedures of intervention that could focus productively on them at the personal level. Social workers have found the concept of systems useful for describing certain patterns of interaction.[5] Anderson and Carter have recently attempted to integrate all phenomena of interest to social workers in a hierarchy of systems.[6]

The concept of a boundary as an aspect of a system and the notion of constant exchange across this boundary help to delineate a more focused target for social work intervention in the environment of the individual. Hearn has described a role for a social worker as a boundary worker.[7] However, these concepts are often too abstract to be easily and directly applied in an actual situation. One cannot really "see" a boundary between an individual and the environment or between groups. Nor are the parts that can be identified within a system usually as clearly interdependent and as clearly directed to a general goal as systems theory would imply.

*Primary group* is a term that has been used to describe an individual's close, personalized contacts. Used in its original context as a way of distinguishing relationships of this type from impersonal secondary ones, it is useful. However, there is a tendency to equate primary groups with more commonly understood groups and to think of them as having commonly held definitions of membership and regular meeting times as a collectivity. A nuclear family fits this description but most groups involving personal contacts between friends, neighbors, and others do not. Terms such as *social circle* and *action set* are looser in connotation but have generally been used to describe friendship patterns and political activity.

We think that using the concept of network as an analytical tool focuses attention on real relationships between real people in a way that suggests both useful information and appropriate intervention for social workers. Unfortunately, because the term is new, there is still a great deal of fuzziness about the concept, and research has barely proceeded from the descriptive stage. In 1969 Mitchell presented a number of studies of networks in African cities and towns. The anthropologists who conducted these studies met frequently during the course of them to compare findings and refine terms. In two introductory chapters Mitchell and Barnes attempted to derive general descriptive terms from research done up to that time.[8] The two authors disagreed in some respects about the proper use of some terms, but out of their work and the more recent work of Craven and Wellman consensus is emerging about several useful dimensions of networks.

## TYPES AND ASPECTS OF NETWORKS

Networks can be *personal networks* (described from the perspective of any individual member) or *general networks* (described from the perspective of an outside observer). A personal network can include persons who are connected through intermediaries to the *central figure* or anchor person. Since networks do not have boundaries, either type could eventually ramify until it included an entire population. Therefore, in describing a general network, authors delimit it by some arbitrary boundary such as all the individuals in a particular village or all who interact with each other during a certain period of time. In describing a personal network, similar limitations are made in describing the number of indirect contacts (that is, those made through at least one other person) that a particular individual (usually called Ego in the studies) has with others. Most individuals are involved in networks of relationships that increase geometrically, and thus it is easy to see that data collection can quickly mushroom. Some authors have relied on the information that Ego provides as to his contacts, while others have tried to pursue these contacts, using a snowball technique, to explore the reciprocal definitions of the relationships. Such research is extremely time-consuming. Fortunately, mathematical techniques derived from graph theory and matrix algebra can be used to simplify the data.[9]

Craven and Wellman describe three aspects of networks that are theoretically useful: (1) density, (2) range, and (3) pathways. Barnes and Bott describe networks as close knit and loose knit. If all the relationships in a network are known, its *density* can be expressed as the ratio of actual links in the network to potential ones. *Range* refers to the number of individuals involved in the network. Range and density can vary independently. A *path,* which constitutes an indirect link between one individual and another through at least one intermediary, can be an important access to resources outside of Ego's immediate circle of contacts. Furthermore, as Craven and Wellman note:

> Knowledge of the membership of a network is not a prerequisite for membership in that network. Upon meeting for the first time, members who have been up to that point only indirectly linked in the network may find that they have many friends or acquaintances in common and have been, unawares, sharing information, norms and values for a long time.[10]

Mitchell listed several other aspects of networks that have not been defined as clearly or elaborated on as much as the foregoing ones: content, directedness, durability, intensity of interaction, and frequency of interaction. These concepts refer to the nature of the links in the network rather than the structural properties of the network itself. We will be concerned with the first two of these aspects when we turn to a more specific consideration of helping networks. It may be that durability, intensity, and frequency are difficult to define because they are more subjective and intertwined. A network's durability is especially hard to study because the passage of time introduces enormous complications in data collection. Several longitudinal studies of helping networks are explained in detail later: the day care neighbor project, the single-room-occupancy hotels, and the rural Kansas project.[11] Other examples of helping networks that are described in this book represent cross-sectional slices. Even the reports of networks observed for more than three years do not deal in detail with changes over time. The relationships between these variable aspects of networks are extremely important from a practical as well as a theoretical standpoint. Social workers would find it useful, for example, to know whether greater intensity and frequency of interaction had increased or decreased a network's durability and to know under what conditions such a change occurred. Unfortunately, research in this area is still in the beginning stage. Craven and Wellman have summarized as follows the generalizations that current research seems to support about how these variables are related:

1. Relatively dense networks are generally small, and the linkages among the members quite strong.

2. Loosely knit networks tend to be large, and their members less deeply involved with one another.

3. In general, large, loosely knit networks appear to expedite access to tangible resources, while dense networks with strong ties expedite access to intangible, emotional resources. However, loosely knit networks sometimes supply more intangible resources in an emergency or a crisis situation.[12]

## *URBAN VERSUS RURAL*

Before proceeding to study helping networks more directly, it is appropriate to examine this question: In modern, urbanized society are such networks rapidly becoming anachronistic? At this point, it should be noted that even if networks were a largely rural phenomena, they would be useful to social workers concerned with rural populations. However, the bulk of this country's population and the bulk of social service activity are located in urban areas. Extended families, folk healers, wise elders, quilting bees, and barn raisings are recognized as important among primitive peoples and in rural societies, past and present. But many would insist that such groups, individuals, and shared community activities are not characteristic of urban life.

Wirth has suggested that typically rural networks disappear as people move from the farm to the cities and as immigrants leave their ghettos and merge into the "melting pot." [13] Indeed, it has been assumed that alienation is the norm and that modular relationships are replacing the *gemeinschaft* of village life.[14] Perhaps the American cult of individualism and the love of change for its own sake also reinforce the tendency to see all relationships as temporary.

The extended family, in particular, had been thought to be a disappearing phenomenon and may be examined as an extreme case. However, researchers who have taken a careful look at the behavior of people who live in cities have found that contacts among kin persist.[15] Many people still prefer to live near their relatives and see them frequently. Even more people see relatives as primary sources of help in crises, and developments in communication and transportation have made such expectations realistic, even across great distances. Calls for help can be relayed via the telephone in minutes and, more important, airplanes can transport the needed person across the United States in less than a day. Studies are seldom able to measure the subtle security that such easy communication may bring to widely scattered relatives. Some writers have encouraged social workers to look upon relatives as a resource for helping families.[16]

Studies of the migration of people from rural to urban environments offer additional evidence that ties of kinship and friendship are important.[17] People do not enter the city as individuals. Often friends and relatives in the city have induced them to migrate. The executive who is transferred to another town has the corporate structure in the new town to help him integrate into the community. When people announce their intention to move, friends and relatives frequently supply them with names and addresses of persons to contact in the new place.

Slums that were initially described, from the outside, as disorganized and atomistic have been found to possess rich networks and systems of social order.[18] Even skid-row districts are now seen to provide much more interaction than was once thought. Bell and Boat, for instance, found that 44 percent of the men in such a district had contacts more than once a week with friends, relatives, or neighbors. Almost one-third of them had frequent contacts with relatives.[19] If so much contact among relatives persists in the most difficult urban conditions, it should not be surprising that urbanites enjoy even richer contacts with non-relatives. The unconnected, alienated urban dweller and the isolated nuclear family can be seen to be more myth than fact.

What is probably true about an urban area—and what sociologists like Wirth may have actually intended to highlight—is that contacts are more numerous and varied than they are in rural areas. In addition to the rather close-knit networks of kin, co-workers, and friends that urbanites have in common with villagers, city dwellers also have opportunities to participate in a wide variety of loose-knit networks. They are also affected by more institutional and impersonal relationships. They have opportunities to develop networks with specialized functions and to keep their memberships separate and, to some extent, known only to themselves. The option of not participating in networks may also be more real in a city, although every village or rural area has its recluses. In the city, however, these isolated persons would be more numerous and therefore possibly more noticeable.

Craven and Wellman argue that, far from being on the wane, networks are growing stronger and that they are necessary to knit cities together and make them function.

> The continued existence of large cities as centers of interaction is not an anachronistic relic of the horse-and-buggy past; rather, the city is a superior milieu for diverse network processes which continue to make it a vital center in the networks of regions, nations and the world.[20]

Kadushin gives an excellent example of how networks can function when he tells how they created a receptive climate and obtained patients for psychoanalysts who migrated to this country in large numbers in the twenties and thirties.[21]

Individuals can and usually do belong to a number of networks at the same time. Networks can be based on kinship, friendship, employment, recreation, education, politics, ethnicity, religion, or whatever other interests or elements people find in common. The content of exchanges can also be varied. An individual may have one network of people who are likely tennis partners, one consisting of people who might contribute to a cause, and another made up of persons whose advice might be sought when buying a house. The nature of the exchanges and the purpose of the network can change over time. Stages in the life cycle obviously make for change as the years pass. All these intricacies complicate the description of actual networks.

## *HELPING NETWORKS*

Fortunately, our concern as social workers is a practical one, so that we can narrow our focus to helping networks and, more specifically, to those generally perceived to assist in a positive direction, namely, those that increase the successful functioning of the individual helped. Viewpoints may differ as to what constitutes a positive direction. Even assuming a general consensus on what is positive and what is negative, it must be recognized that many negative networks exist, such as those between alcoholics who aid each other's dependence on the drug. Social workers are well aware of these negative networks. Juvenile court counselors, for example, are often heard to say, "My kid would be all right if he weren't influenced by the others he hangs around with." The irony is that every other member of the gang probably has a counselor who feels the same way. Negative networks will not be discussed in this book, but it is important for social workers to understand them better. They deserve to be given attention in the future, when they may be seen in a different light, as serving necessary as well as asocial functions for their members—functions that must be replaced if these networks are destroyed.

Informal, spontaneous helping activities occur so often all around us that they usually pass without notice. Except for spectacular rescues, instances of helping behavior are much less likely to be reported than are instances when bystanders failed to act on behalf of someone in distress. Witness the wide coverage of murders when observers did not become involved in aiding the victim, even to the extent of calling the police. Social workers are trained to notice instances when people fail to receive help or support from those in their normal circle of acquaintance. Formal social welfare services have been developed to compensate for breakdowns in informal problem-solving processes. There is a danger, however, that the social worker may become absorbed in organizing and maintaining formal services and be blind to the informal, positive, helping activities that go on constantly outside the confines of formal services. Were it not for the informal services of helping networks, social agencies—whether they recognize it or not—would be swamped. Besides carrying the bulk of the service load in many sectors (for example, day care, home care for the elderly, and temporary foster care), helping networks also carry out a widespread preventive program. They offer accessible, individualized services that formal agencies could never match. Considering the important role these networks play, it is especially unfortunate that social workers often consider their services as "competition" provided by unprofessional persons whose motives are questionable.

Some of the illustrations that follow will be of networks in which mutual aid is clearly the dominant mode of interaction. Networks of mutual aid are pervasive and of course are of basic importance. Other illustrations involve relationships in which the mutuality of the exchange is not as obvious. In these, direction is vital. In many networks, helping activities seem to flow mainly in one direction. The helper does not receive a direct repayment in kind for the effort put forth. Networks that involve a primary caregiving person—whom we have called a central figure or natural neighbor—are less understood, and they offer professional social workers great potential for sensitive collaboration. By identifying a central figure, the social worker can come to understand a complex network of relationships through a single contact. Collaboration therefore can be highly efficient.

## CENTRAL FIGURES

Who are these central figures? We have identified several types of persons who are likely to be natural neighbors. Probably the most stereotyped example is the home-centered woman who plays a central role for other families in similar circumstances in her neighborhood. Most of us have probably recognized persons who fill the same kind of role in places other than residential neighborhoods—for instance, in factories, offices, dormitories, and army barracks. These are not persons carrying their role because a title or a position gives them their importance. Rather, they have won the confidence of their associates because of their personal characteristics, and they have demonstrated their ability to cope successfully with problems similar to those that their co-workers or neighbors face.

Some central figures have a job or a role that brings them into contact with people who need help. Their interactions with these people—who may perhaps be clients, customers, or tenants—far exceed those required by their job. Of course, many people in these particular occupations do not extend themselves in this manner. Bartenders and beauticians have received some publicity about performing helping activities. However, various other occupations offer similar opportunities. For example, grocery checkers may be important contacts for some individuals.[22] Customers often have favorite checkers who maintain a continuing interest in their lives, going beyond polite chatter. We have observed grocery checkers and druggists who were the centers of complex networks of elderly persons. They actively watched over the well-being of their aged customers and enlisted the concern of other customers in their welfare.

Guernsey described in a newspaper article the importance of a gas meter reader to isolated families in rugged hill country.[23] The article noted that he is "friend, counselor, chaplain and social worker" to his customers. He has arranged for hospitalization for an injured customer, done community relations work when a black family moved into a "redneck" area, and mobilized neighbors to build an addition on the house of a crippled retiree. In another article Guernsey described a custodian at a community college who is a "Dear Abby" for the students.[24] College administrators recognized that her contribution was vital, transferred her to the cafeteria where she would have even more contact with students, and instructed the deans to pay special attention to her requests for assistance.

Even relatively infrequent contacts that are usually casual and limited to a specific role such as those between a neighborhood resident and the owner of a gas station or a dry cleaning establishment can be important sources of support and human warmth in urban neighborhoods.[25] Jacobs believes that such contacts are essential to the safety and viability of neighborhoods.[26]

What motivates individuals to involve themselves with others? This question, seldom put to professionals, is inevitably asked when the existence of natural networks is discussed and the possibility of social work relationships with them is proposed. And it would be useful to answer the question, since social workers are interested in fostering such activities.

The question has been approached from several angles. Unfortunately there is no definitive answer. The elements motivating prosocial behavior, the conditions promoting altruistic attitudes and the environmental factors conducive to helping acts are all subjects that must be examined; as yet they have not been studied thoroughly.[27]

It has long been recognized that societies are held together by a network of reciprocity.[28] Individuals help others to insure that they, in turn, will receive help when they need it. Since this behavior is functional for society it is supported by social norms.[29] This broad explanation does not fit many specific situations, however, nor does it explain why some individuals are more inclined to be helpful than others. Part of the explanation may be that the mutuality involved is more subtle than a tit-for-tat reciprocity. Thus the helper's reward may not be obvious but is none the less effective in monitoring helpfulness. Of course, different people respond to different rewards. Societies also have norms that may conflict with the norm of reciprocity under specific circumstances, forcing the individual to make a choice.

Psychodynamic theory would see such helping behavior depending largely on the personal characteristics of the helping person. Extending help to others demonstrates basic trust and what Erikson calls "generativity." [30] Mutual relationships involve balancing dependence and independence.

A series of ingenious experiments in the laboratory and in natural settings recently explored the situational factors influencing prosocial behavior.[31] It was found that whether an individual will be helpful to another is influenced by the context of the situation, the presence or absence of an authority figure or of other bystanders, and the presence or absence of helping models. These factors are probably more important in emergencies involving strangers than under more stable conditions in which the individuals have a continuing relationship.[32]

Physical factors too can be conducive or detrimental to helping behavior. Both Jacobs and Newman have studied and described physical conditions that will foster neighbors' active concern for each other.[33] Others have noted that residents of new housing developments tend to make friends first with the people living close to them if they have much in common.[34] Physical conditions can make contacts practically impossible or, on the other hand, almost unavoidable. (Consider the extreme case of a crowded elevator stopped between floors.) Just because contacts take place, however, does not necessarily mean that positive helping networks will develop.

Our experience leads us to believe that personal traits provide the most likely explanation for the development of central figures whose helping activities persist over long periods of time. We summarize these traits in the concept "freedom from drain." This phrase denotes that the individual who undertakes to be a central figure does so without fear or danger of depleting his own emotional or physical resources or without the hope of replenishing them. Rather, the role is undertaken because of mature concern for others. Thus, central figures are likely to be individuals who are sufficiently on top of their own life situations, and sufficiently rewarded by them, to be able to give to others and be responsive to others' needs. Some central figures may also be motivated strongly by guilt or by neurotic needs—such as the need to make others dependent on them—but we believe that these persons are exceptions. In any case, our primary focus is not on therapeutic change of the central figure but on increasing that person's usefulness in helping networks.

The need for future research on the nature and functioning of networks in general and helping networks in particular seems obvious. Social workers of course have been doing field research on helping networks since the profession began. One reason for writing this book is to encourage social workers to share their insights with professionals in other disciplines and begin to use the analytical approach toward networks, which promises to be so useful. Enough is already known about networks to indicate their tremendous potential for social work. They exist as semipermanent social structures in all cultures, in cities as well as villages, among people of every class. Their importance for social order and integration may increase rather than diminish as society becomes more complex. Networks are one of the most vital bridges between the individual and the environment. Helping networks are the informal counterpart to organized social services and in many areas carry the largest part of the service load. Since helping networks respond directly to consumer needs and preferences, they can give social workers much useful information for planning formal service programs. Finally, since many networks contain central figures, productive relationships between social workers and these central figures can dramatically extend the effective reach of professional efforts.

## Notes and References


1. Paul Craven and Barry Wellman, "The Network City," *Sociological Inquiry*, 43: 3 and 4 (1973), pp. 57–88.
2. John A. Barnes, "Class and Committees in a Norwegian Island Parish," *Human Relations*, 7 (February 1954), p. 43.
3. Elizabeth Bott, *Family and Social Network* (2d ed.: London, England: Tavistock Publications, 1971).
4. J. Clyde Mitchell, "The Concept and Use of Social Networks," in Mitchell, ed., *Social Networks in Urban Situations* (Manchester, England: University of Manchester Press, 1969), pp. 1–50.
5. Gordon Hearn, ed., *The General Systems Approach: Contributions Toward an Holistic Conception of Social Work* (New York: Council on Social Work Education, 1969).
6. Ralph E. Anderson and Irl E. Carter, *Human Behavior in the Social Environment* (Chicago: Aldine Publishing Co., 1974).
7. Gordon Hearn, "Social Work as Boundary Work," *Iowa Journal of Social Work*, 3 (Spring 1970).
8. John A. Barnes, "Networks and Political Process," in J. Clyde Mitchell, ed., *Social Networks in Urban Situations*, pp. 51–74; and Mitchell, "The Concept and Use of Social Networks."
9. Craven and Wellman, op. cit., pp. 60–61.
10. Ibid., pp. 68–69.
11. Arthur C. Emlen and Eunice L. Watson, *Matchmaking in Neighborhood Day Care* (Corvallis, Ore.: DCE Books, 1971); Joan Shapiro, "Dominant Leaders Among Slum Hotel Residents," *American Journal of Orthopsychiatry*, 39 (July 1969), pp. 644–650; and Shirley L. Patterson and Esther E. Twente, "Utilization of Human Resources for Mental Health," Final Report (Lawrence, Kans.: School of Social Welfare, University of Kansas, 1972) (mimeographed).

12. Craven and Wellman, op. cit., pp. 73–74.
13. Louis Wirth, "Urbanism as a Way of Life," *American Journal of Sociology,* 44 (July 1938), pp. 3–24.
14. Alvin Toffler, *Future Shock* (New York: Random House, 1970).
15. Herbert Gans, "Planning and Social Life: Friendship and Neighbor Relations in Suburban Communities," *Journal of the American Institute of Planners,* 27 (May 1961), pp. 134–140; Michael Young and Peter Willmott, *Family and Kinship in East London* (2d ed.; Harmondsworth, Middlesex, England: Penguin, 1962); Bott, op. cit.; Wendell Bell and Marion D. Boat, "Urban Neighborhoods and Informal Social Relations," *American Journal of Sociology,* 52 (January 1957); Eugene Litwak and Ivan Szelenyi, "Primary Group Structures and Their Functions: Kin, Neighbors, and Friends," *American Sociological Review,* 34 (1969), pp. 465–481; J. P. Sutliffe and B. D. Crabbe, "Incidence and Degrees of Friendship in Urban and Rural Areas," *Social Forces,* 42 (October 1965), pp. 60–67; Phillip Fellin and Eugene Litwak, "The Neighborhood in Urban American Society," *Social Work,* 13 (July 1968), pp. 72–80.
16. Marvin B. Sussman and Lee Burchinall, "Kin Family Network: Unheralded Structure in Current Conceptualizations of Family Functioning," *Marriage and Family Living,* 24 (August 1962), pp. 231–240; and Hope Jensen Leichter and William Mitchell, *Kinship and Casework* (New York: Russell Sage Foundation, 1967).
17. Craven and Wellman, op. cit., p. 70.
18. Gerald Suttles, *The Social Order of the Slum* (Chicago: University of Chicago Press, 1968); and Young and Willmott, op. cit.
19. Bell and Boat, op. cit., p. 394.
20. Craven and Wellman, op. cit., p. 84.
21. Charles Kadushin, "The Friends and Supporters of Psychotherapy: On Social Circles in Urban Life," *American Sociological Review,* 31 (December 1966), pp. 786–802.
22. Esther Peterson, "The View from the Checkout Counter," *Parade,* 22 (July 1973), pp. 13–14.
23. John Guernsey, "Meter Reader Strong Friend," *Sunday Oregonian,* Portland, Oregon, September 23, 1973.
24. John Guernsey, "PCC Custodian 'Dear Abby,'" *Oregonian,* Portland, Oregon, September 1, 1973.
25. Gerald Caplan, *Support Systems and Community Mental Health* (New York: Behavioral Publications, 1973).
26. Jane Jacobs, *The Death and Life of Great American Cities* (New York: Random House, 1961).

27. Dennis L. Krebs, "Altruism—An Examination of the Concept and a Review of the Literature," *Psychological Bulletin*, 73 (April 1970), pp. 258–302.
28. Petr Kropotkin, *Mutual Aid* (Boston: Extending Horizons Books, 1914).
29. Alvin Gouldner, "The Norm of Reciprocity: A Preliminary Statement," *American Sociological Review*, 25 (April 1960).
30. Erik H. Erikson, *Identity, Youth and Crisis* (New York: W. W. Norton & Co., 1968).
31. J. R. Macaulay and L. Berkowitz, eds., *Altruism and Helping Behavior* (New York: Academic Press, 1970).
32. Lawrence S. Wrightsman and John C. Brigham, eds., *Contemporary Issues in Social Psychology* (2d ed.; Monterey, Calif.: Brooks/Cole Publishing Co., 1973), p. 130.
33. Jacobs, op. cit.; and Oscar Newman, *Defensible Space: Crime Prevention Through Urban Design* (New York: Macmillan Co., 1972).
34. Leon Festinger, Stanley Schacter, and Kurt Bach, *Social Pressures in Informal Groups: A Study of Human Factors in Housing* (Stanford, Calif.: Stanford University Press, 1950); and Gans, op. cit.

# 2

# Networks and Social Work in the Past

As we reviewed social science literature pertaining to our field of interest, we recognized that we had not really made a discovery when we had noted the existence of viable natural networks, but rather had rediscovered a phenomenon temporarily buried from view but nevertheless intact and functioning. Then, as we looked over our own professional past, we realized that we and other social workers have had a variety of contacts with natural networks over the years. In this chapter we will attempt to sketch social work interaction with natural networks in the past, painting a broad picture that can only show some of the major avenues of approach and must ignore the byroads and bypaths explored by our professional colleagues of an earlier era.

The early social workers were volunteers who drew on the long human tradition of helping through natural networks of kith and kin when they began to reach out to assist those who were not so related to them. Indeed, since they described themselves as "friendly visitors," it might be conjectured that many of those pioneers were familiar, from personal experience, with the functions carried out by natural neighbors, or central figures in natural networks, and that their social work activities merely extended the network activities.[1]

The pioneering model was a more active one than most social workers would feel comfortable with today. A century ago natural neighbors did not confine themselves to helping those who asked for assistance, either in their own extended families or in their rural neighborhoods. They took it upon themselves to offer help and advice when they thought it was needed, whether because of stress at a time of crisis or because of chronic failure to conform to community standards. They scolded as well as praised, threatened punishment by man and God, and often gave generously from their own resources or mobilized the resources of others.

In a sequence frequently reenacted when social work began to develop as a profession, the first contacts made between the helping people and the strangers they offered to help tended to turn the thoughts of social work leaders to more efficient ways to help and ways to extend needed services beyond their personal reach. Among the people served were war casualties, newcomers to cities, migrants or immigrants, and physically or emotionally handicapped children and adults.

Children's institutions were organized to care for the orphaned, other children without families who could care for them, and those whose families were considered unfit to give them care that would assure their growing up to an independent and upright maturity. The institutions were expected to serve as surrogate families. Plans for cottage living were developed that, it was believed, would give the children the benefit of growing up in a subculture that reflected national standards and aspirations. But attempts to create artificial networks for a specific purpose were rarely successful. Staff members employed to act *in loco parentis* were inevitably preoccupied with maintaining order, meeting the needs for the children's upkeep, and assuring their own positions. Although, in many instances, staff members served as substitute parents to individual children, few attempted to develop positive networks of relationship involving themselves, the children, and the community. In fact, the isolated geographic position of most institutions—particularly those for delinquent children—reflected the community's rejection of these children without families, which was difficult to overcome. However, separate networks grew up within the institutions, which served to knit the youngsters together in an alliance whose purposes were survival and protection against the adults officially designated to help. The adult caretakers often built their own networks to protect themselves from the youngsters and the outside community. The interaction between these networks embodied the least supportive as well as the most supportive aspects of kinship systems, intensified by the isolation of both networks from participation in healthier community systems. "Asylums" organized to deal with other deviant individuals developed similar patterns.

## *THE SETTLEMENT MOVEMENT*

The settlement movement had quite a different approach toward assuring a better future for the entire community. Its pioneers recognized the need for social reform if individual inequities were to be adjusted and community standards upheld and improved. To accomplish these ends, they believed that they themselves should be in closer contact with those who needed better living conditions so that they might teach them and support their efforts. Founders of the settlement movement carried out their convictions by leaving their own upper-middle-class settings and becoming neighbors in every sense to those they saw as needing their help in the slums. "Neighbor" and "neighborhood" and discussions of mutuality are found on every page of the literature of this period.[2] The settlement social workers made an effort to relate to the neighborhood residents at times of family celebration and success as well as times of crisis. They used existing networks of group interaction to achieve what they believed to be a primary objective—helping neighbors improve their social condition. Clubs based on ethnic models brought from other cultures were invited to meet at the neighborhood houses. These small natural peer networks were, as they had always been, centers for the exchange of information and mutual help in the personal lives of members and their families. In addition, the clubs transmitted the process of acculturation which social work leaders considered desirable.

Social workers could also gain insight into social problems at first hand by fitting themselves into natural neighborhood networks. As they became aware of needs, social workers took on the role of spokesmen for social reform. They enlisted members of the natural networks as disciples, hoping to guide them in acquiring the skills necessary to achieve social change. It was assumed by workers and by many slum residents as well that attaining an education and being assimilated into the mainstream of American life would lead the residents toward success. Residents and workers alike agreed that young people must be encouraged to strive toward these goals even though their efforts might take them away from their natural networks of kith and kin.

In fact, these goals were largely achieved, and many workers in neighborhood settlement houses eventually found themselves out of touch with dynamic natural networks.[3] Their role became, in the main, a supporting one, helping less ambitious and more handicapped people in the neighborhood and the new waves of immigrants and migrants who were excluded from the general upward mobility. The predominantly volunteer character of the first settlement movement diminished; volunteers were generally replaced by part- or full-time paid staff in most settlement houses. For some years, activities were largely recreational with little attention devoted either to natural networks or social reform.

With the growing knowledge about individual differences and psychological processes and, at the same time, social workers' increased education, the focus on the individual in need of help became intensified in all social work practice. As professional social work service became more costly and as large sums of public as well as private funds had to be justified, time-saving office interviews generally replaced neighborhood visiting. Social workers were less concerned than they had been previously about seeking out those in need and offering them services. They were occupied with attempting to meet the increased demand for services, generated by their growing expertise and by programs of assistance they had helped to institute. Since they were removed from actual physical and visual contact with their clients' subcultures, whether ghetto or suburb, most social workers—not surprisingly—concentrated their attention for a time on individuals and almost completely lost sight of the networks in which the clients moved.

## COMMUNITY ORGANIZERS

Paradoxically, some social reforms achieved during the early years of the century created a need for a new kind of community leader—the community organizer who could influence the large bureaucratic institutions growing up in the social services and the complicated political forces controlling them. Community organizers began to view their role as helping natural neighbors to understand processes and strategies that would make them effective change agents. But natural neighbors are characteristically preoccupied with more immediate problems—the care of children and the elderly, assistance at times of family crisis, advice and support to a small circle of friends and acquaintances. For the most part, natural neighbors, whatever their socioeconomic level, did not respond to efforts to involve them in less personal spheres of influence. Most of them who were successfully recruited into community organization activities probably were not true natural neighbors or perceived as such by their networks but were, instead, closer to what political scientists call opinion leaders or influentials.[4] This is a distinction we consider important and one that is easily overlooked.

During the past twenty years, natural networks have once again been seen for what they are, and social workers have made greater efforts to become involved with them. External pressures for greater return on investment in social services as well as a professional desire to implement theoretical findings in the social sciences have no doubt contributed to this renewed interest. The general public, although it had come to accept the responsibility of providing for those unable to care for themselves, became increasingly appalled at the number of people needing such assistance and at the spiralling cost of services. Professionals in all the human services began to recognize that increased knowledge of personality deviation and advances in treatment skills had expanded the potentialities for providing constructive services, but adequate manpower and funds to provide them were lacking. Social science theory uncovered new perspectives on groups and systems that seemed to promise a way out of the impasse.[5] Studies undertaken by social scientists began to point to the existence of both natural and artificial networks that might be further explored.

Delinquent adolescents became a highly visible population of great concern to the general public at all times because of the threat to property and to the value system of the majority. In the 1950s this threat became increasingly intolerable as delinquent gangs, always a feature of large cities, took on racially charged overtones and moved farther out of slum neighborhoods to threaten the middle class. Action was demanded to protect the public and to avoid the enormous expense of constructing institutions to house more and more offenders.

Insights into systems theory stimulated social work to move toward intervening with gang networks, revising the efforts of an earlier generation of social workers who had invited natural networks into buildings under their direction. Social workers sought out natural gang networks "on the street" and attempted to establish a relationship which would influence their members to conform more closely to the standards of the larger community and to behave in ways that would lead to more satisfying lives. The workers recognized that their efforts could only be successful if channeled through the central figures of the natural gangs. Conventional professional techniques were modified to this end, and the new techniques developed to reach out to groups who had not asked for social work intervention were found useful in practice with individuals.[6]

## MENTAL HEALTH

Institutional networks were also studied in the 1950s, especially those in mental hospitals—again because of mounting public concern with constantly rising costs and because professionals believed that new knowledge should be applied to bring about more effective intervention. Studies of mental institutions showed that artificial networks were operating there against the best interests of both staff and patients, in a manner reminiscent of the early children's institutions.[7] This research led to a reexamination of the effects of institutionalization and to a growing conviction that our prisons, reformatories, and mental hospitals did more harm than good in many cases. Social workers, as members of mental health teams, participated in such studies and in subsequent efforts to change the way that the artificial networks operated so that the operation was more like that of the therapeutic community.[8] But it was clear that such a process would be slow and only partially successful at best in meeting the public demand for lower costs and greater efficiency and in satisfying professional concern for the improved functioning of individuals.

At about this time. practice in social work and other disciplines in the mental health field began to be reconsidered in the light of the developing theory of preventive intervention based on public health concepts. Another concept—environmental influence—was also affecting practice in the mental health field. From the start of the child guidance movement early in the century, it had been recognized that environment had an important influence on the individual's mental health. Clinics had added social workers to their staffs expressly to investigate and interpret to professionals of other disciplines the effects of the patient's environment and to suggest needed environmental changes.

Although environmental influence was seen largely in relation to the immediate family, social workers recognized that the school, the church, and recreational and cultural groups were important and must be involved. Contacts with these institutions or groups were usually made through individuals having an official and traditional role. In schools in particular, but also in other host settings, social workers concentrated on treating individuals directly in the setting and on training non-social work staff in case-finding and referral. Many attempts were made to coordinate treatment with the efforts of other caretakers, but neither natural nor artificial networks were directly involved in the treatment process.

Applying principles of preventive medicine to human services, especially in the field of mental health, stimulated examination of service delivery. According to public health theory, preventive efforts were seen as a continuum in which three main levels might be distinguished.[9] At the primary level, efforts were made to prevent the development of illness by protecting people from noxious elements that might cause it. At the secondary level, illness was in its early stages and efforts focused on providing prompt treatment to prevent serious consequences. At the tertiary level, serious illness was present and efforts concentrated on preventing permanent impairment or death. Mental health professionals realized that crisis intervention had great potential and had demonstrated that it was vital to intervene promptly at times of crisis.[10] When social workers examined their own practice, they realized that they operated chiefly at the secondary and tertiary levels.[11] This recognition, together with such major national developments as civil rights legislation, revitalized social work concern and involvement in moves to improve the total environment. The convictions grew in some circles that only through environmental change could primary prevention be assured. Concern with the total environment led to renewed interest in discovering natural leaders in disadvantaged populations with whom social workers might collaborate. The aim would be to help these natural leaders promote broad social action that would change the conditions of their own lives and those of their neighbors. Katz, among others, has described such efforts well.[12]

For a time, it was believed that the rate of success could be increased and the cost of social services reduced if all the professionals dealing with a multiproblem family were brought together to form a helping network.[13] Much effort was expended and countless meetings were held to determine which agency or individual might best act as a kind of natural neighbor with a particular family, but there was little evidence that this approach was successful. Perhaps one reason for its relative failure lay in the mistaken idea that such uneasy alliances could be forged into working networks and that the arbitrary nomination of a central figure would, in fact, create a professional natural neighbor.

It was logical that the theory of preventive intervention was most directly applied by professionals in mental health services, because the theory itself had originated in that field and pressure for change was strong. Mental hospitals were recognized to be at the tertiary level of intervention, and it was clear that more attention to delivery of services was needed at the primary and secondary levels. However, it was also recognized that existing services fell far short of meeting individual needs in the present and could not hope to meet them in the future. Systems theory drew attention to the environment and its primary as well as secondary preventive potential.

Because of their essential roles, teachers, nurses, clergymen, and the police were all viewed as central to networks that are the modern continuation or equivalent of kith and kin networks. In this case the individuals were seen by themselves and by others as official caretakers in a specialized area; at the same time, they might be making use of services that others supplied in a different area. Could social workers develop a new kind of relationship to such systems? Since social workers and their non-social work colleagues who are the specialized caretakers share concern about the well-being of network members, why not enter into a relationship of mutuality on behalf of network members? Translated into practice terms, this meant that social workers would attempt to reinforce the positive interactions between teachers and pupils, public health nurses and patients, ministers and parishioners. They would limit their own intervention with network members to efforts undertaken through official caretakers. They would intervene only in response to a caretaker's requests for help, which might be made at any preventive level, including a crisis.

This preventive approach was successful in situations in which (1) a relatively well-understood social structure surrounded the network and (2) both the social work consultants and the caretaker consultees (that is, the professionals involved in schools, hospitals, parishes) were familiar with the demands and hierarchy of the culture. Difficulties arose in the use of this approach and in the delivery of services by other means when social workers were attempting to reach the hitherto underserved populations that the large, federally funded antipoverty programs of the 1960s brought sharply into focus. It became clear that if these needy populations were to be assisted, the professionals seeking to serve them must first understand the cultures and subcultures. Also, a way must be found to bridge the abyss of unfamiliarity and distrust that separated the existing neighborhood networks from the professionals designated to help the people solve their problems.

## INDIGENOUS LEADERS

The means to achieve this end were modeled more closely on the current community organization approach than on consultation, but there were unique features too. An effort was made to identify indigenous leaders who had a central position in their cultural networks and to recruit them into the agency systems of service delivery. They were trained in agency procedures both as a means of reaching the natural networks and as a step toward their achievement of career goals.

In some instances, after periods of difficulty, the desired goals were attained.[14] But in many instances the professional staff was dissatisfied with the performance of the indigenous recruits who, in turn, felt that they were indeed bridges—walked on from both directions by the professionals and by their own former network members.[15] The cost for many of these indigenous leaders was unquestionably high, since they lost status in the natural neighborhoods and yet encountered practical obstacles to true career opportunity within the established hierarchies of agencies.

Professionals, too, found this approach unexpectedly disturbing. In some instances, when they became closely acquainted with indigenous workers, the professionals—greatly impressed with the high degree of natural skill and with these workers' ability to intervene effectively—went so far as to conclude that formal professional training should be abandoned. Some even maintained that professionals should, for the most part, abdicate in favor of these untrained natural neighbors.[16] Others drew the opposite conclusion—that untrained people were ineffective—perhaps as a consequence of the federal mandate directed toward eliminating dependence through the creation of new careers.

These programs reflected another trend of the times in requiring that consumers of service be given a voice in policy-making and planning. Here again, it was unclear who should be chosen to share in these functions, and although some natural neighbors undoubtedly were selected, many other individuals having no such network position served in these capacities.[17]

Although there is a voluminous literature on impressions about the techniques and the outcomes of incorporating indigenous individuals into agency staff, little of it is truly evaluative, especially with respect to the effects of training.[18] The problems created by long bureaucratic lines of communication, the capricious assignment of funds, the unsettling effects of changes in rules and regulations imposed on local programs, and the general air of impermanence have all been described elsewhere, and all unquestionably had a destructive impact on these programs. But despite all the negatives, there were tremendous gains in the degree to which social workers came to recognize the extent and variety of natural networks through direct contact with them, and to realize their potential in preventive intervention. It is possible even now, to discern and describe some of the ways in which these new insights are influencing social work practice in relation to natural systems and to discuss some of the methodology that emerged.

Looking back, then, over the history of social work collaboration with natural systems, it can be seen that there was a constantly developing if not always visible trend. Not surprisingly perhaps, the development has not been logical or linear. Social workers have at times lost sight of the goals and methods of the early settlement house workers as they responded to new definitions of problems, changing conditions, increased knowledge, and changing political priorities. But their fundamental concern for the person-in-the-situation has brought them back again and again to neighborhoods, natural networks, and natural neighbors.

## Notes and References

1. Nathan E. Cohen, *Social Work in the American Tradition* (New York: Holt, Rinehart & Winston, 1958).
2. Jane Addams, *Twenty Years at Hull-House* (New York: Macmillan Co., 1910); Robert A. Woods, *The Neighborhood in Nation-Building* (New York: Arno Press, 1923); and Stanton Coit, *The Soul of America* (New York: Macmillan Co., 1914).
3. Herbert Gans, *The Urban Villagers* (New York: Free Press, 1962).
4. George Brager, "The Indigenous Worker: A New Approach to the Social Work Technician," *Social Work*, 10 (April 1965), pp. 33–40; and James A. Kent, *Death of Colonialism in Health Programs for the Urban Poor* (Denver, Colo.: Foundation for Urban and Neighborhood Improvement, 1972).
5. Gordon Hearn, ed., *The General Systems Approach: Contributions Toward an Holistic Conception of Social Work* (New York: Council on Social Work Education, 1969).
6. Otto Pollak, "Treatment of Character Disorders: A Dilemma in Casework Culture," *Social Service Review*, 35 (June 1961), pp. 127–134; and Alice H. Collins and James R. Mackay, "Casework Treatment of Delinquents Who Use the Defense of Denial," in Francis J. Turner, ed., *Differential Diagnosis and Treatment in Social Work* (New York: Free Press, 1968).
7. Erving Goffman, Asylums: *Essays on the Social Situation of Mental Patients* (Chicago: Aldine Publishing Co., 1970).

8. Maxwell Jones, *The Therapeutic Community: A New Treatment Method in Psychiatry* (New York: Basic Books, 1953).
9. Gerald Caplan, *Principles of Preventive Psychiatry* (New York: Basic Books, 1964).
10. Howard J. Parad, ed., *Crisis Intervention* (New York: Family Service Association of America, 1965).
11. Cohen, op. cit.
12. Alfred H. Katz, "Self-Help Organizations and Volunteer Participation in Social Welfare," *Social Work,* 15 (January 1970), pp. 51–60.
13. Bradley Buell, *Community Planning for Human Services* (New York: Columbia University Press, 1952); and Ludwig L. Geismar, *Understanding the Multi-Problem Family* (New York: Association Press, 1964).
14. Alan Gartner, *Para-Professionals and Their Performance* (New York: Praeger Publishers, 1971).
15. Philip Kramer, "The Indigenous Worker: Hometowner, Striver, or Activist," *Social Work,* 17 (January 1972), pp. 43–49.
16. Harry Specht, Arthur Hawkins, Floyd McGee, "Excerpts from the Casebooks of Subprofessional Workers: The Neighborhood Subprofessional Worker," *Children,* 15 (January 1968), pp. 7–16.
17. Kent, op. cit.
18. Alan Gartner, op. cit.; and Charles Grosser, William E. Henry, and John Kelly, *Nonprofessionals in the Human Services* (San Francisco: Jossey-Bass, 1969).

# 3

# Some Natural Networks Described

As we explored the possibilities of working with natural systems, we collected every report we could find about similar social work projects, finding a sparse but interesting literature that we could compare and contrast with what we were doing and with the attitudes and techniques we considered necessary for successful intervention. In preparing to write this book, we intensified our efforts and included a wider professional range of authors, including not only authors in social work but those in all the health professions. Our search was hampered by the lack of a common terminology and a common conceptual base for the social phenomena that were of interest to us. Consequently, we cannot claim to have taken into account all the useful descriptions of helping networks available in the literature. In fact, we are continually happening upon new projects—some by happenstance or word of mouth—that are building on natural networks. It is frustrating to know that much useful information is slipping through our fingers, but every new discovery increases our belief in the timeliness of the approach. A second problem caused by the lack of a common terminology and conceptual base is that we may sometimes be guilty of reinterpreting others' findings in ways which they would not have foreseen. To this charge, we can only plead that we have tried to be as faithful to the original reports as we could in terms of descriptive data, and we take the responsibility for our interpretation of them. In the following chapters we describe many of these reports, make brief comments about them from our relatively narrow and specialized position, and frankly express our personal judgments about their relationship to more traditional approaches and the probable success of their techniques.

A major organizational puzzle for us has been how to present the projects according to a logical scheme of categorization. We have grouped them loosely under chapter headings, but we are aware that this is an arbitrary device for greater readability rather than a rigorous attempt at classification. Categorizing projects according to the type of network, the professionals' objectives, the means of observation and intervention must some day be undertaken but this lies in the future. In the meantime we have grouped and discussed projects in a way that seems logical to us and hopefully will to the reader.

If professionals are to work with natural helping networks, they must become aware of the kind of networks that exist and understand what part they play in the lives of their participants. It should be recognized that these networks provide generally supportive subcultures for their members and that specific relationships develop between network members and certain central network figures.

To help familiarize more social workers with existing networks, we will discuss some networks that involve individuals who are known to need many services but who are not usually being reached by the traditional system of service delivery. We hope that these examples will not only be new and informative, but also will bring flashes of recognition and will illuminate familiar, firsthand experience. We believe that, fundamentally, there is no substitute for actual contact with persons involved in helping networks.

## *TAVERN CULTURE*

Dumont has described an unrecognized natural network among a population almost as foreign to most social workers as peoples in remote places described by anthropologists—the "tavern culture" of homeless men.[1] Because of his concern for public health, Dumont wanted to find a means of reaching these men who "cling to the underside of every major city." He decided to study them as a patron and observer in a bar frequented by skid-row men, responding with friendliness to their overtures and watching their interaction with each other and with Peter the bartender. He noted that Peter, who also was the proprietor of a boarding house for single men, had a central position in the network. Men frequented the bar only when he was there, asked him to handle their welfare checks, borrowed money from him when they were broke, and accepted his regulation of their drinking and their "pesty" manners. Peter differentiated his role as bartender from his roles as friend and landlord, but he was sensitive to the emotional and physical needs of the men and willing to invest time and effort in meeting them.

Dumont noted that the tavern offered the men the only "home" they had, a place that gave them a sense of belonging and the physical comfort their lives otherwise lacked. Since they had long been alienated from their families and had little or no identity as part of a labor force, these men had only each other as a reference group. The bar was a place where they could talk to each other and, tangentially, to Peter about the past and their cheerless present. Peter was the central figure who knit the men into a network.

In spite of his resolve to act only as an observer, Dumont, as a physician, could not resist attempting to improve the health of the men by supplying Peter with some vitamins and asking him to dispense them regularly. Dumont concluded:

> The barroom hangout of homeless men does not exist only to exploit and aggravate social pathology. It performs a life-sustaining function for men who have literally nothing else. It may provide their only opportunity for a tolerant and supportive environment, for socialization, for rest and warmth.
>
> When urban designers reach the stage of planning for these men as well as for the more established poor, they will have much to learn from the taverns. In the meantime, those health professionals who already feel a responsibility to deal with the well-being of all people should not pass up the opportunity to use taverns as outposts.[2]

## *SRO RESIDENTS*

Shapiro has described a population more varied in age and sex but no less isolated from society.[3] Their many physical and emotional disabilities bring them sporadically to the attention of professionals but, in general, their relationships with formal services are marked by mutual distrust, fear, and watchfulness.

Shapiro and her staff in the community psychiatry department of a large hospital that has a number of single-room-occupancy (SRO) buildings in its neighborhood undertook to understand these tenants and serve them more effectively.

It was found that within each building the tenants formed small groups which served them like families—caring for them when they were drunk, under the influence of drugs, or otherwise ill; sharing money and material things; and providing companionship for drinking and card-playing. These groups, which were made up of seriously disturbed individuals, were subject to many disruptions, quarrels, knife-playing incidents, accusations, and counteraccusations. In some, the dominant individuals exploited group members. But central figures were often present who provided a degree of stability and cohesion. As Shapiro noted, "A recurrent pattern is the matriarchal quasi-family in which the dominant woman tends to feed, protect, punish, and set norms for 'family' members."[4] She went on to describe three leaders who

> . . . wield unusual personal influence and engage in activities analogous to those of the mental health worker. These three have a large and stable following in their respective buildings, and they function within the power thus bestowed upon them to support, nurture, heal, and sometimes infantilize those in their care, in effect being a "good mother" to a highly dependent group of physically and emotionally ill people. In the microcosm of the SRO, these three leaders have a high level of energy, the capacity to negotiate the world outside, and to remain active and resourceful in the face of poverty in comparison to their followers. The latter, in turn, vastly enhance the power of the leader, not only because of the reality-based protective, feeding, and controlling functions she provides but also by the parental omnipotence with which they endow her.[5]

In spite of severe physical and emotional problems of their own, the leaders had in common

> . . . vivid, expressive, and forceful personalities; they tend to show a wide range of emotion—love, pity, anger, remorse, empathy, and humor—to those in their "family" and to outsiders to whom they have built a close relationship. They establish rapport with outside sources of power whenever possible; personal contact is made with the local policemen, welfare in-

vestigators, managers, and other service people on whom the tenants depend. Sometimes a mutual bargaining develops between the leader and these people, a by-product of which is better service to the tenants.[6]

Each also had her own special style of relating to her network. Among other things, Mrs. Johnson nursed the sick members and, when she felt they needed hospitalization, saw to it that an ambulance was called to take them to the hospital. She protected their belongings and took care of their welfare checks in their absence and helped to reestablish them on their return. Mrs. Crawford was especially skilled in mediating for members of her network with such organizations as the welfare department, seeing to it that they received all the benefits they were entitled to. Mrs. Smith had a supply of psychiatric drugs that she doled out to severely disturbed tenants. She encouraged those who had returned from mental hospitals to take their prescribed drugs. Over the years she had developed a good relationship with the admitting clerk at the hospital nearby who was ordinarily somewhat hostile to alcoholic patients but who would admit those Mrs. Smith sent in.

Shapiro points out how these leaders are useful:

> The SRO leaders' usefulness seems to lie neither in the political arena nor in the service organizations. They are frequently too vulnerable and eccentric to tolerate job frustrations, and too debilitated physically for full-time regular employment. Also, there is little incentive for many of them to give up their positions of authority in their buildings to fill low-status positions in a professional world.
>
> The majority of the leaders are valuable precisely because they live and work, albeit haphazardly, with a community of unrecognized patients who, in the usual course of events, would never be seen by a psychiatrist. They perform an invaluable service, for as far as they are able, they mitigate potential disorganization in response to stress and reduce disturbed behavior and neighborhood blight. They are, in fact, the unpaid and invisible staff of nameless and unendowed halfway houses—the SROs. That such altruism can exist at all under circumstances which often produce greed, that within an intolerable living situation the creation of a quasi-family can occur, is a tribute to the human being's boundless adaptive capacity to find and use others in his struggle for survival.[7]

## A MEXICAN-AMERICAN COMMUNITY

In an article pointing out that a conventional mental health clinic in an urban community failed to reach Mexican Americans, Torrey describes some of the natural helpers who already serve such communities.[8] The *curanderos*, who have a long tradition of healing by magical as well as practical means, are consulted by individuals who are obviously mentally ill as well as by others who have interpersonal problems, such as marital difficulties. Although Mexican-American communities know the *curanderos* well and the people often consult them instead of consulting "Anglo" agencies, or in addition to consulting these agencies, these helpers are rarely discussed with outsiders, and they do not identify themselves for fear of persecution by the police.

Torrey warns that true *curanderos* should not be confused with those who use that title but are in fact fortune-tellers. He indicates an important difference: the fortune-tellers charge set fees and appear to be mainly interested in "extracting as much money as possible from their patients"; true *curanderos* accept whatever is given to them.

In a Mexican-American community there is another group of helping people who have no title and who serve as advisers on an entirely voluntary basis. They have no training as healers but have gained an informal reputation as problem-solvers. Torrey identified twenty such central figures in a relatively small urban community, and he describes several of them. Other residents see these figures as persons to turn to when they have a problem. These helping people have regular jobs that they work at daily, but they devote many evening and weekend hours to counseling those who ask them for help. Sometimes they visit the homes of troubled residents, at other times receive them into their own homes, advising on problems that range from schizophrenia to marital discord. Torrey reports the techniques of one of these individuals as listening and ventilating and quotes her own remarks that describe what she does in contrast to the practice of highly trained professionals:

> "I listen mostly. Then they often feel better. Sometimes they understand what's going on better just by telling me. I also encourage them to express their feelings. They're scared to. I tell them I know it will be hard at first."

Some of Mrs. P's empathy is a product of her own past domestic difficulties. At one point she sought traditional Anglo psychiatric help. Its failure typifies the reason why she is a major mental health resource for the Mexican-American community:

"I couldn't talk to him. All he ever did was ask me about things way in the past. My problem was in the present. I couldn't talk to him at all." [9]

## *MENTAL HEALTH PROGRAM*

Mental hospitals have been reducing their populations in recent years by moving many long-term patients into community facilities. Boarding homes have become a major type of housing for these ex-patients. Boarding-home providers are paid with public funds for the care they provide. However, they are not employees of the hospital involved or of the welfare department, but are independent entrepreneurs who choose to care for this specialized population and do so with minimal supervision and no formal training.

One of the authors of this book was part of a team of community mental health workers who collected data about the providers and residents of boarding homes in a neighborhood that was heavily loaded with such facilities.[10] The workers were interested in learning what the arrangements were in the boarding homes, how the providers viewed their tasks, what the physical surroundings were, and what the average length of stay was in a home. The long-term goal was to plan a program for providers that would improve the care given the residents. From contacts with fifty-two boarding homes that housed over three hundred patients a composite picture was drawn showing the typical provider to be

> a woman about 60 years of age with extensive previous work experience in a caretaking occupation such as practical nursing, cooking or foster care. She has been married but is now widowed or divorced. Her stated reasons for becoming a home provider and specializing in the care of mentally handicapped persons are a combination of needing extra income, liking people and wanting to help people.

As a group, the home providers are independent, energetic, maternal women, who often grow large vegetable gardens and have many indoor plants as well. They can their own food and do most of the maintenance work around the homes themselves. Talkative and hospitable to anyone who comes to their homes, they tend not to be involved in activities in the larger community. Most had never seen the state mental hospital thirty miles away. While they feel the public looks down on them for "running a boarding house" and "living off other people's checks like parasites," they also feel that they are performing a real service in helping their residents adjust to the community and in meeting their needs for care. They live with the residents twenty-four hours a day and, except for shopping which is a major activity, seldom leave the home.[11]

Far from finding that the boarding homes were a social evil, the mental health workers found them to be a tremendous resource. They learned to admire the boarding-home providers who were often furnishing mental health services with native skill. Their report concludes:

> While we did encounter two or three grossly substandard and unscrupulous home providers, we were generally impressed with the quality of care and the dedication of the home providers. The real nucleus of the home care system consisted of the women described above. With no formal training and little encouragement from agencies but with a great deal of understanding and experience in living, they have created an occupation. Significantly, many of these women are known to one another and in frequent communication by telephone. They recruit other suitable providers into the business, give each other advice about food, problems with their boarders and a host of other matters and "pass the word" about troublesome residents or agency personnel. Their boarders tend to have a lower rehospitalization rate than those of home providers who do not take a personal interest in or spend time with their residents or see the home solely as a source of income rather than a satisfying vocation.[12]

These reports of networks have common features of considerable significance. The central figures are, in every sense, volunteers in their helping capacity. Although the bartenders and the boarding-home providers carry on their helping roles concurrently with their employment, the assistance they provide is not part of their job descriptions. They do not ask or expect advice or help from professionals in rendering this service. Some deliberately avoid contact with organized services; others understand the value of formal services for network members and mobilize them on behalf of those who need them. Although some central figures are themselves agency clients, this does not intrude into their network position.

The natural neighbors described in these reports differ in the degree of interaction they stimulate within their networks. Their helping styles differ according to their sex, their settings, and their individual personalities. But they are alike in their spontaneous response to the needs of others and in their willingness to listen and act on their behalf. They do not view themselves as "doing anything," yet, at every preventive level, they reach individuals who are not reached by professional social workers. They take on the responsibility of the helping role willingly and carry it out consistently and conscientiously over time, making use of everything they can learn to improve their performance. Professionals who come in contact with them (for example, those who wrote the descriptive accounts quoted in this book) may approach them initially with skepticism but often soon become admirers and advocates of their efforts. In short, as central figures in neighborhood networks, these people perform unique and important human services, and they qualify as colleagues in a partnership with social workers no less than nurses or teachers.

## Notes and References

1. Matthew P. Dumont, MD, "Tavern Culture: The Sustenance of Homeless Men," *American Journal of Orthopsychiatry*, 37 (October 1967), pp. 938–945.
2. Ibid., p. 944–945.
3. Joan Shapiro, "Dominant Leaders Among Slum Hotel Residents," *American Journal of Orthopsychiatry*, 39 (July 1969), pp. 644–650.
4. Ibid., p. 646.
5. Ibid., p. 646.
6. Ibid., p. 648.

7. Ibid., p. 649–650.
8. E. Fuller Torrey, "The Irrelevancy of Traditional Mental Health Services for Urban Americans." Paper presented at the annual meeting of the American Orthopsychiatric Association, 1970.
9. Ibid., p. 8.
10. Diane L. Pancoast, "Boarding Home Providers for Released Mental Hospital Patients." Unpublished manuscript, 1970.
11. Ibid., p. 3.
12. Ibid., p. 7.

# 4

# Traditional Approaches to Natural Networks

If it is agreed that natural helping networks exist in areas that social workers are concerned about but seldom reach, then it becomes of major interest to discover a way to reach them. This chapter describes and discusses projects based on traditional social work methods of service delivery: casework, group work, and community organization.

It appears to us that all these projects used natural neighbors in ways that met some of the needs of both the consumers of services and the agencies providing the services. But we believe they did so in a manner that failed to make optimum use of the potential of the natural networks. As had been the case in the past in utilizing volunteers and paraprofessionals, the natural networks were fitted into existing patterns of practice, a procrustean operation obliterating those aspects of natural systems that give them unique value in the total service delivery complex.

## *ALASKAN WELFARE AIDES*

In a report of evaluative research carried on to judge the success of a program using Alaskan natives as public welfare aides, Feldman describes the technique of service delivery.[1] The project had been undertaken as a way to serve a population widely scattered over a huge and hostile terrain. It was known that Alaskan natives often needed basic help in the daily struggle to stay alive as well as advice in dealing with serious accidents, illness, alcoholism, and the effects of a hazardous and unpredictable physical environment. The professional staff members of the public welfare agency recognized that they were unable to meet many of these needs because of distance, cultural and lingual barriers, and lack of time. In an effort to bridge these gaps, the project that Feldman reports was designed and implemented. Natives were selected, trained as public welfare aides, and sent into the field to carry out some of the tasks formerly assigned to caseworkers. The aides were chosen because most of them were

> . . . leaders in their communities—members or presidents of their village councils, former magistrates or other officials, renowned hunters, or persons respected for wisdom and experience. To their HSA [Human Service Aide] roles they brought intimate knowledge of the Native people and villages; understanding of their culture, needs and aspirations; sensitivity to the opportunities and threats of technological changes; and dedication, tempered by practical ingenuity, to increasing the well-being of their fellow villagers.[2]

They were chosen in accordance with certain hypotheses that included the following assumptions:

> Many ways exist for meeting social need; no single method is best for meeting all kinds of problems or even some problems in various cultural or community settings.
>
> The best persons to solve problems in remote and isolated communities might be those with inherent and commonsense capacities for innovation and accommodation to adverse conditions without benefit of supervision by or consultation with others.
>
> There are variations among HSA's and villages and within villages.
>
> The assessment of how social need is met, whether by families or villages, should be sensitive to the reciprocal relationship of the people and their physical environment, a relationship from which their life styles have evolved over centuries and through which certain kinds of strength have endured.[3]

The aides were chosen according to these hypotheses but were then given a nine-month period of training in carrying out public welfare programs. Modeled after those tested in other states and regions, the program consisted of two academic training periods separated by four months of on-the-job training in the villages.

The academic training included planned sequences of formal classroom lectures and discussions along with supervised field observation and experience. A project director, a training supervisor, a supervisor for each group of public welfare aides, and clerical aides made up the project staff. Because of the problems caused by distance, transportation, and weather, conventional supervision was not possible once the period of training was over and the aides began their work in the remote villages. These public welfare aides made the required reports in writing. However, English was a foreign language for most of them and their formal education was limited. Thus the reports were merely brief statements of action taken to carry out their tasks according to the agency's requirements.

Evaluations of the aides' performance reported that they did indeed use innovative techniques. Rather than following the usual agency practices, they made judgments about needs according to their own cultural standards, and they saw to it that the needs were met through the use of agency resources. In a sense, they reversed the expected process. They incorporated some of what they had been taught into their network roles, rather than using their network status and know-how in carrying out agency procedures and objectives.

The welfare aides did not show any interest in the social work role of bringing about social change to alleviate problems that their clients faced. Nor did they undertake any activity along this line. Rather, they continued to act on their age-old knowledge that the harsh environment narrowly limited the possibility for change and that the pressing need was to meet the casualties of daily life that this environment imposed. It has been noted in various studies that natural neighbors are usually more interested in providing practical immediate help than in attaining long-range social goals.[4]

It seems clear that the Alaskan native project aimed to incorporate into a conventional casework program some of the knowledge of local life and customs through the natives recruited to serve as paraprofessional public welfare aides. In evaluating the program it appeared at first glance that, in the main, this goal had been achieved. But a closer look detects that the aides continued to function in their customary roles in the natural network, utilizing appropriate procedures to help their friends and families to a greater extent than had previously been possible. Being remote and inaccessible to supervision enabled them to make these modifications and prevented the co-optation that has occurred in most projects.

## A GHETTO PROJECT

"Intervention in two natural social systems . . . without requiring people to perceive themselves as patients" was the objective of a group work project carried out under the auspices of a mental health clinic in a black ghetto, which Taber described.[5] The project was based on the hypothesis that ghetto residents' low self-image and sense of powerlessness could best be understood and influenced to change for the better by an "ecological systems approach." Taber explains it as follows:

> The ecological systems approach directs our attention to the transactions and communications which take place between individual members of the poor black population and the systems within and outside their neighborhood. . . . Our explorations of these transactions, or "interfaces between systems," shows that most of the transactions which take place are degrading and demoralizing, and are experienced by the ghetto resident as "put downs." [6]

Intervention was directed at two natural systems—a group of families living on a street where there were many social problems and an adolescent gang. Taber noted:

> Unlike members of an artificial group, members of a natural group have day-to-day contacts and ongoing significance in each other's lives. . . . We sought to work with natural systems without requiring that the people perceive themselves as patients. The intervenor sought to define his role as that of advisor rather than leader or therapist.[7]

A parent group was formed, with the view of improving child-rearing practices. Indigenous community workers introduced the mental health professional to people in the neighborhood. They helped to form and maintain the group, which slowly began to function as parent groups in other settings do. The group elected officers, planned social and educational events for themselves and their families, and finally became involved in improving the community. One of the leader's objectives was to include men in the group, but this was not achieved. Apparently having male members in a parent group was too far from the neighborhood norm to be accepted, even though the group did undertake activities that were not the usual ones of the natural system in the street.

The other natural group with which the clinic staff began to intervene was a loose gang of high school boys who were far behind in school but who had no major violations of the law in their police records. They were invited to meet regularly at the clinic with the mental health professional and to bring their friends. "The initial ten-meeting program focused on current relationships with school, police, and community, on vocation and the development of black pride and awareness, on sex and parenthood." [8]

The interventor suggested that, instead of merely tape-recording their discussions, the boys might make recordings about life in the ghetto.

> The group picked this up enthusiastically as an opportunity of showing people outside the neighborhood some of the positive things about themselves, since they thought the papers usually talked about the bad things. . . . It became possible to highlight and underline examples of positive coping.[9]

The group soon decided to become a club, the intervenor took on the role of adviser, and the boys initiated a variety of constructive tasks—for instance, planning and holding dances, forming a basketball team, starting an odd-job service (that later involved furniture-moving contracts), writing articles for the clinic newsletter, and making program presentations to the clinic staff and the sponsoring agency's board of directors.

If this account were read without knowledge of its mental health milieu and the views of the staff on ecological systems, the reader well versed in social work history might well assume that it was an illustration drawn from the early settlement house literature or from the era of street work. In fact, the worker took more initiative than might have been the case in many more conventional approaches of group work in that he did not simply offer his help to an already organized group. Instead, he used the boys in a loose junior street gang as a nucleus, stimulated them to recruit other boys, and helped them to become an agency-based, socially acceptable club carrying out constructive tasks. And, although the boys met in their own neighborhood, they did so in a setting unfamiliar to them and followed an agenda proposed by the worker. The discussion topics too—with the exception of sex—were not natural to the group. The worker reports that the "group structured itself" but it might be more accurate to say that the group made use of the structure developed to carry out projects he proposed.

Since the worker was based in a mental health center and was presumably trained mainly in that specialty, it is possible that he was unfamiliar with the history and techniques of social group work and so was not aware of "having invented the wheel." And it is also notable that the "wheel" of social group work is indeed a useful invention and can serve in many ways, including that reported here!

Nevertheless, it must be noted that if either the mothers on the block or the loose gang of boys had been a strong natural network with a central figure, the strategies described would probably have made little contribution to the network. Indeed, professional intervention might inadvertently have denigrated the potential of the central figure and limited that figure's ability to function by substituting a professional who acted as organizer, director, and leader of a different model.

Another danger of using conventional group techniques with natural networks is that the group worker may not distinguish between networks that have a negative effect on their members and those that have a positive one. There is almost no evidence that consultation with negative systems is effective, and it can often put the social worker who attempts it in a dangerous and illegal situation. The failure that at present seems inevitable with negative systems may contaminate efforts to work with positive natural systems and may lead to the conclusion that all work with natural systems is unprofitable, a consequence we consider so damaging in the current stage of this method's development that we feel it essential to express this *caveat.*

## A MEXICAN-AMERICAN HEALTH CENTER

Most community action programs of the 1960s attempted to involve residents of the target area and were successful in doing so to a greater or lesser degree. One of the most interesting and well-described efforts was the establishment of a health center in a poor Mexican-American neighborhood of Denver, Colorado, carried on by Kent and his associates. This program took into account Mexican-American customs and existing networks in the neighborhood to be served.[10] Careful study of the neighborhood and its natural caretakers led to the development of principles for working with such groups. These principles, in the main, were derived from on-the-spot observation and interaction between those persons—professional and nonprofessional—who helped bring about change, and the people whom the program served.

The philosophy of health underlying the group's community organization efforts is that "health is a total community process —a total life process." [11] Thus those responsible for the undertaking believed that they could not deal with diseases alone, but had to deal with all the factors and conditions that interrupted or detracted from the physical or mental health of the individuals in the neighborhood.

The first step that the professionals took followed Freire's approach.[12] They observed and talked with neighborhood people about their routine activities, and then helped these people describe how they managed their lives. Setting aside stereotypes, these professionals discovered and reflected back to the people what their situation really looked like. This process clarified individual and neighborhood problems both for the professionals and the population to be served and helped the people develop their own guidelines for living and acting. Descriptions covered physical, social, and economic realities and led to plans for organizing services that would truly meet deficiencies of the community while building on its inherent strengths.

The project staff found a building for a health clinic that was literally in the natural pathways of the community. They proceeded to redesign the health clinic to accord with the preferences elicited from the residents. For instance—because the people feared and distrusted secret places and wanted to see what was happening to everybody—the physicians worked in a circular open area, record-keeping was done in the open, the medical laboratory and the dental laboratory were both visible.

Some neighborhood residents were recruited for the agency staff and given responsibility for assisting with its budget and for managing business ventures that grew out of the health program, such as the transportation system for patients. Many Chicano residents had come to know and trust the staff members through the health center, and thus talked with them quite freely about neighborhood problems. These residents pointed out that housing was a crucial need, and staff worked with them to improve it. Staff members saw themselves as leading the fight against the establishment in order to surmount the obstacles that deterred the Chicanos from achieving their housing goals. Through projects such as these—projects that grew out of the staff's understanding of community needs and wants and that were led by staff experts, including physicians and lawyers—a number of new cooperatives were organized. They were related to vital areas of everyday life—health, work, housing, and transportation.

The professionals, in the course of their work, came to know the natural caretakers. Some were *curanderos* like those mentioned in the Torrey article; others had assumed various helping roles with adults and children in the community. Kent sums up his way of work by saying:

> We are domesticated and if we don't free ourselves from domestication, we can't really be helpful to others to free themselves. We have to be able to go out and look at what's happening in a culture, describe it, and use that description in designing a health system that fits that culture. That is cultural action for freedom in co-learning with people; using professional skills when they're needed, but not imposing those skills when they're not. It's being in that natural process with them through reflection—figuring out what we really did, that enables us to build a concept out of that action. There is a very real distinction between cultural action for domestication and cultural action for freedom.[13]

Although Jane Addams and all the community organization professionals who came after her might not have stated their goals in Kent's colorful language, they would have been likely to see their objectives in the same light and to believe that they were achieving them through their own methods.

Upon reviewing the projects described in this chapter, it seems evident that they did indeed fit the natural networks into existing patterns of practice. The Alaskan natives, who were chosen because of their understanding and position within their own culture, were trained to take their place at the bottom of the public welfare professional hierarchy. The loose gang of ghetto boys, who might or might not have constituted a natural network, was converted into the time-honored club within an agency that was itself alien to their neighborhood. The natural neighbors who had for years cared for their fellow Mexican-Americans were enlisted to establish a service, certainly a service badly needed and sensitively planned, but nevertheless one that superseded them and diminished their influence and their power —no matter how good the intentions of the organizers.

When natural neighbors are viewed chiefly as an innovative avenue for delivering traditional services, it is not surprising that they are adapted to these services, either as providers or recipients within a well-tested and time-honored model. Before proceeding to use natural neighbors in such ways, social workers should review other possible approaches, since natural helping networks are apt to be fragile when confronted with powerful outside forces, natural neighbors are sensitive to put-downs, and approaches that damage these systems are probably not reversible.

# Notes and References

1. Frances Lomas Feldman, "Reaching Rural Alaskan Natives Through Human Service Aides," *Welfare in Review*, 9 (May/June 1971).
2. Ibid., p. 10.
3. Ibid., p. 11.
4. *See*, for example, Philip Kramer, "The Indigenous Worker: Hometowner, Striver, or Activist?" *Social Work*, 17 (January 1972), pp. 43–49.
5. Richard Taber, "A Systems Approach to the Delivery of Mental Health Services in Black Ghettos," *American Journal of Orthopsychiatry*, 40 (July 1970), pp. 702–709.
6. Ibid., p. 703.
7. Ibid., pp. 705–706.
8. Ibid., p. 704.
9. Ibid., p. 707.

10. James A. Kent, "A Descriptive Approach to a Community." Unpublished paper, 1973.
11. Ibid., p. 1.
12. Paolo Freire, *Pedagogy of the Oppressed,* Myra B. Ramos, trans. (New York: Seabury Press, 1972).
13. Kent, op. cit., pp. 25–26.

# 5

# Artificial Networks Organized to Meet Needs

Recognition that natural neighbors have unique qualities and that many individuals in modern society need the kind of support and feedback which natural neighbors offer has led to some interesting projects. These involved the organization of artificial networks that would take on the functions of natural ones. We believe that artificial networks tend to be most viable and feasible when they replace those that operated similarly under other conditions, when natural neighbors already exist even though they function minimally, and when the natural neighbor is readily accessible to the potential clients.

The impetus for developing artificial networks came from the theory of crisis intervention, which holds that the outcome of crisis in an individual's life largely depends on the help immediately available when crises occur.[1] In settled communities this help was most often given in the past by a member of the extended family or a close neighbor or friend. In modern urban societies, clergymen, physicians, and sometimes law enforcement officers are seen as official caretakers who—if family and friends are not present—take their place. The role of professional social workers has been described as consulting with and supporting these caretakers.[2] But many crises occur when neither relatives, friends, nor official caretakers are available. Various means are being tested to create artificial systems that will go on to function as natural systems.

## WIDOW-TO-WIDOW PROGRAM

One such project was the widow-to-widow program that Silverman organized under the direction of Dr. Gerald Caplan at the Laboratory for Community Psychiatry at Harvard University.[3] It followed a number of studies on bereavement and agency involvement with bereaved individuals, a population known to be at risk in terms of severe emotional disturbances and found to be largely unserved. Especially important were the young widows who had experienced the untimely death of a spouse.

The program was predicated on an understanding of the sequence of emotional transitions after bereavement and on correlation of intervention with the various stages of bereavement so that it might be as effective as possible. Preliminary studies had found that neither mental health agencies nor those in other fields reached widows, in part because widows did not present a defined psychiatric disorder and in part because they did not turn to such agencies for help. The widows interviewed did not regard friends, family physicians, and clergymen as helpful because these people tended either to avoid them or urge them to "keep a stiff upper lip at a time when the widows felt their lives were ended and any hope for the future gone."[4] The widows felt that their best help came from other widows. The young ones, however, had a special problem. Young widows and their families were likely to live in neighborhoods with other young families who had not known such bereavement, so that the comforting contacts other widows could offer were not readily available.

To remedy this situation, the widow-to-widow program, after defining the target population and the areas, recruited widows living nearby to contact the recently widowed, who were identified through municipal death records and funeral homes. The recruits, called aides, were chosen for their activity in their own neighborhoods and their demonstrated capacity to care about others rather than for their educational background. They were encouraged to initiate contacts with the newly widowed, to visit them and listen to them. Subjects of greatest importance to the newly widowed were the loss of the husband and feelings of helplessness and anxiety about the future. It was an ongoing program, aiming to explore continuously the kinds of services needed and to facilitate the aides' work of helping these newly widowed women build networks of people who would provide new social contacts and supports.

This artificially organized widow-to-widow network replicates a natural one that functions with a minimum of professional intervention in rural societies and in some urban apartment houses for the elderly. It would appear that one test of the viability of such a project would in fact be its longevity and increasing independence.

A project like this should not be confused with another kind of network that Caplan calls a "specialist" system.[5] A common misfortune or need holds individuals together in such a system—for example, in Alcoholics Anonymous, the many other organizations on that model, and the associations of parents of the mentally retarded or emotionally disturbed. These groups come together so that members may support each other in the face of a chronic problem, console each other in mutual experiences of pain, encourage each other by providing examples of successful coping, and make a concerted demand that their needs be considered. They are focused on an objective rather than on the many levels of interpersonal relationships of the generalist natural networks. Although such groups rarely avail themselves of professional services and are often hostile to professional intervention, their leaders use the same basic techniques as do community organizers. It will be interesting in the future to study the differences and similarities between specialist and generalist natural systems and to differentiate appropriate means of professional intervention with them. This book will deal, however, with generalist networks only.

## *NURSES AS CRISIS COUNSELORS*

The procedures followed in the widow-to-widow program were virtually reversed in a crisis-counseling project in Vermont that focused on the prevention of suicide.[6] Professionals—registered nurses in this instance—who lived in rural communities were asked to take on an informal counseling role in addition to their professional one. Actually, the nurses were chosen because they were already functioning as central figures in community health delivery. The project director queried community leaders as to which nurses were known to respond to their neighbors' cries for help, and he then selected the thirty-five most often mentioned. These nurses were trained briefly in the fundamentals of psychiatry, and the training included recognition of the symptoms of suicidal intent and effective intervention for such cases.

The women were not given extra pay for their work as crisis counselors but continued to act in the voluntary capacity familiar to them. Unlike the widow aides, all the nurses had similar education and professional experience. However, an ability to listen sympathetically and a willingness to respond promptly to need, both as an expert and as a friend, were determining qualifications for the choice of these "crisis counselors," not education. The program was regarded as a low-cost, informal, neighborly project that would offer help to emotionally disturbed people during a crisis, in the absence of a trained psychiatrist. The emergency counseling role of the nurses was not publicized.

> To ensure privacy and inspire confidence in the needy, Dr. Marshall made no public announcement of the nurses' availability, yet word-of-mouth soon caused their practices to flourish.
>
> There are no set schedules or office hours for the crisis-corps' nurses—they're on call day and night, wherever they may be. People stop them on the street to discuss a problem, call them at home or stop by for a chat.[7]

The nurses were able to offer vital support and encouragement to persons facing serious physical and emotional problems—for instance, family members of terminally ill patients or individuals overwhelmed by anxiety. They were also able to give practical advice on health problems and to interpret medical procedures that had been misunderstood and thus had caused minor crises.

> Though the prime function of the corps is to de-fuse crisis situations, they do not abandon their patients when the first storm is over. Further help continues in visits once or twice a week—for months if necessary. Any patient found to require intensive, professional psychiatric care is immediately referred to the nearest mental-health clinic. The nurses work closely with the clinics, and even then follow up the patient when he is discharged.[8]

During its first four years, the crisis corps helped to prevent seventy suicides and helped more than a thousand emotionally disturbed people to cope with emergencies of many types. The report at the end of that period noted:

> Not one of the 35 nurses originally enrolled in the corps has dropped out. . . . When asked whether payment to the nurses might not inspire them to even greater efforts, Dr. Marshall's reply is an emphatic, "No!"
>
> "The value of this program," he says, "lies in that very thing—its voluntary character. People seek the help of crisis nurses as they would that of friends and neighbors. We feel we'd sacrifice a good deal of that confidence if the nurses were paid for their services."
>
> And as for the nurses themselves [one of them], the mother of four, speaks for all of them when she candidly admits that, though she could use the money, "I couldn't accept it. Honestly I'd feel guilty if I were paid for being a good neighbor." [9]

## *YOUNG AND OLD TOGETHER*

Ellis describes an artificial network organized in response to the need that social workers had observed in two community populations.[10] The two—widely different in age but alike in being alone too much—were elderly people living in the comparative isolation that is more or less natural to their time of life and children who were unnaturally isolated from their peers and their families.

The project took place in a community in which many mothers worked to contribute essential family income. Thus a large number of "latch key" children came home from school to an empty house and were alone until one parent or the other returned at the end of the workday. These children tended to become withdrawn and silent.

Those who counseled the elderly in this community had observed that two factors were likely to be present: "insufficient monthly income to meet basic needs and despondency, usually triggered through death or inactivity." [11] Social workers believed that both the children and the old people were suffering from loneliness, having few people to listen to or talk with them. Could the withdrawal of the young and the despondency of the old be lessened by bringing the two together? A program designed to meet the needs of both groups was planned. The program's objective was to create an artificial network between the children and the elderly people that would provide mutually satisfying relationships and stimulating activities and would also encourage the development of peer networks in both groups.

An after-school, recreational activity was set up, with the older people staffing small informal centers where the children could come for a snack that their elderly hosts provided. There would be plenty of opportunity for interaction between young and old, and the centers would also be places where the boys and girls could meet others their own age and join them in indoor and outdoor games and crafts. The ratio of children to oldsters was maintained at six to one so that each child would always have the chance and the time to talk and be heard and for the oldsters to relate to them. A project director and a secretary were employed to take care of the practical tasks of finding space, arranging for food delivery, and so on, but the oldsters in each center were encouraged to plan and carry out a program in accordance with their skills and the children's interests.

> Activities are emphasized as vehicles for relationships with the secondary gain being the achievement of a finished product as in a craft or the winning of a game in play. Feeding, because of the emotional implications in filling up emptiness in withdrawing behavior of children, was emphasized in all centers.[12]

The teams of oldsters assigned to serve as staff for the centers were selected in an especially interesting manner. The basic requirements for being accepted into the program were that the applicants should be over 55 years of age, in good health, emotionally stable, interested in children, and willing to work for the minimum wage—at that time, $1.60 an hour. Elderly persons interested were invited to a series of training sessions consisting of lectures and task-oriented groups. The staff teams for each center were chosen by observing the natural groups that developed during the training period.

> The success of the project is measured in the children's continuing to come to the centers and the fact that 75 percent of the original applicants are still employed.
>
> At the conclusion of the first year of the project 100 percent said looking forward to working on the project added interest to their life and broadened their ideas and interests. Fifty

percent listed the love of the children and 33 percent stated making friends with other oldsters as an important gain for them.[13]

It might be noted that, as in the widow-to-widow program, the project was planned and carried forward through the efforts of professionals. However, once organized, every effort was made to encourage the development of a network closely resembling that of the extended family of an earlier time.

## PEER COUNSELING IN A SCHOOL

A project described by Hamburg and Varenhorst was more ambitious in its goals and procedures than the others described in this chapter, since it not only involved certain individuals in the community but was tailored to the complex setting of a secondary school.[14] The rationale for the project was described as follows:

> The modern American nuclear family with its smallness, mobility and relative isolation from other kinship ties has need of a network of non-familial supports. The schools have become the social institution which would appear to have the necessary ingredients for playing a major role in meeting these needs. The role of teachers and counselors as parent surrogates can be clearly seen. The role of students as surrogates, models, bridging persons and sources of useful information for each other has been somewhat overlooked.
>
> Some prior work has shown the value of using peers in tutorial and/or counseling roles with other students. However, the bulk of such efforts have been at the college level. We wished to see the principle extended to the secondary schools. Therefore, we undertook to devise a program of peer counseling which would utilize students in grades 7–12 (ages 12 through 18 years). . . . Present counseling and guidance services are inadequate both in terms of manpower effectiveness and also in terms of acceptability to a significant percentage of students. Furthermore, it seems important to also reach out to less troubled students with preventative approaches. This latter student is almost never seen by a busy counselor.[15]

A program was planned in which student counselors would be recruited and then trained by highly skilled professionals.

It was hoped that this would serve as a pilot program for replication throughout the school system of that city and others.

At first glance, the program seems to depart radically from the foregoing projects that involve artificial networks, and this is true to some extent. Students were not selected according to their place in the natural system but were admitted to the training program without screening. Those planning the project assumed that the not-so-well-suited would drop out during the rigorous training. In fact, obstacles to continuance were deliberately included in the training, with this end in view. Expectations of outcome were extremely ambitious.

> Peer counselors were not conceived of merely as academic tutors but viewed as assistants in solving personal problems; teaching social skills; giving information about jobs, volunteer opportunities and mental health resources in the community; acting as models; developing friendships; acting as a bridge to the adult world for disaffected students; and finally, over a period of time, serving as agents of change where the school atmosphere is characterized by coldness and indifference.[16]

Some of the roles mentioned are natural to adolescents, and individuals may be found in most groups who have chosen to act in some or all these capacities with peers and juniors. However, some roles—for example, making referrals to mental health facilities and counseling students older than themselves—were certainly not a natural part of adolescent functioning.

The program began with a planning committee that was made up of students, parents, teachers, counselors, staff of the school's central office, and the project's codevelopers. After the approval and support of school administrators and parent groups was obtained, a training program that included a variety of exercises and experiences was offered to interested students. It was apparent that the training in itself was helpful to the prospective peer counselors who came to understand themselves better and to develop a greater interest in and commitment to the school and their peers. Hamburg and Varenhorst point out that the demand for peer counselors by widely different groups within the school system indicated that the concept had already been accepted and that the young counselors could be expected to continue to function successfully in the future.

The outcome of this project suggests that it is possible to create a truly artificial network that will operate with success if it effectively meets a perceived need. This instance involved an appreciation of the assistance that young people, given the necessary professional training, might render to promote the mental health of their peers. However, the cost of such undertakings as this peer counselor project would be extremely high, both in time and money, since they involve long periods of training and support by highly skilled professionals. Such training would probably have to be continuous because of the built-in attrition as the aides grow up and have to be replaced. School populations are themselves often highly transient, which adds another obstacle to the continued operation and self-sufficient growth hoped for in such artificial networks as those involved in the first three projects in this chapter.

## Notes and References

1. Lydia Rapoport, "The State of Crisis: Some Theoretical Considerations," in Howard J. Parad, ed., *Crisis Intervention: Selected Readings* (New York: Family Service Association of America, 1965), pp. 22–31.
2. Gerald Caplan, *The Theory and Practice of Mental Health Consultation* (New York: Basic Books, 1970).
3. Phyllis B. Silverman, "The Widow to Widow Program: An Experiment in Preventive Intervention," *Mental Hygiene*, 53 (July 1969), pp. 333–337.
4. Ibid., p. 334.
5. Gerald Caplan, *Support Systems* (New York: Behavioral Publications, 1974).
6. Don Robinson, "On Call for Crisis," *Good Housekeeping* (March 1971), pp. 92, 167–170.
7. Ibid., p. 168.
8. Ibid., p. 170.
9. Ibid., p. 170.
10. June B. Ellis, "Love to Share: A Community Project Tailored by Oldsters for 'Latch-Key' Children." Paper presented at the 49th Annual Meeting of the American Orthopsychiatric Association, Detroit, Michigan, April 1972.

11. Ibid., p. 1.
12. Ibid., p. 5.
13. Ibid., p. 8.
14. Beatrix A. Hamburg and Barbara B. Varenhorst, "Peer Counseling in the Secondary Schools," *American Journal of Orthopsychiatry,* 42 (July 1972), p. 566–581.
15. Ibid., p. 567.
16. Ibid.

# 6

# New Alliances with Natural Networks

As mentioned in the introduction, when we were planning the Day Care Neighbor Service as a project that would use existing natural networks, we could find no reports offering guidance or precedents. Yet projects were going on in widely separated geographic areas, under various auspices and titles, that were being based on hypotheses similar to ours and were arriving at similar conclusions. This chapter presents some of these projects as well as one of our own. All are based on the assumption that there are natural networks with central figures or natural neighbors who are helping people and also coordinating the assistance of others for the benefit of those within their networks. It is assumed that natural neighbors differ from both professional social workers and from customary client groups and that they resemble but are not identical to competent non-mental health professionals, such as nurses, teachers, and ministers. We see natural neighbors as responsive to social workers' offers of collaboration and consultation, and we believe that they can make optimum use of such a relationship.

Most of the projects quoted in this chapter began after a period of study or, at least, of participant observation that was undertaken to discover whether a natural network existed and, if so, how it functioned. The findings were then used as the basis for the careful planning of a project to be carried out with a particular network, adapting the project to the network's idiosyncratic style of functioning. This technique differed from that used in projects previously described, in which professionals noted the importance of natural networks or natural neighbors and then either used them in traditional service delivery or, if the natural systems or neighbors were absent, created artificial systems to compensate for them.

## *EXTENDING INDIGENOUS SERVICE*

A mental health project in Kansas reported by Patterson and Twente was a response to the same kind of difficulties that prompted the organization of the Alaskan native program described in Chapter 4.[1] It took into consideration that provision of services has increasingly focused on large urban areas and the problems compounded by urban life. Thus most federally funded programs of the past decade were based on perceived needs of residents of large cities. Yet despite the well-publicized national trend toward urbanization, a significant proportion of the country's population still lives outside cities and is at present seriously underserved by official agencies. New ways of reaching this population are urgently needed. This Kansas project provided mental health services in a rural area. It grew out of an earlier research and demonstration project, "Mobilization of Aging Resources for Community Service," that was funded for three years by the National Institute of Mental Health and administered by the University of Kansas School of Social Welfare, Lawrence, Kansas.

The project made these basic assumptions: (1) natural neighbors can and do act in a helping capacity, (2) they help in a way which differs from that of professional caretakers of all kinds, and (3) their style should be supported but in no respect altered by training or supervision. The project's setting, objectives, and rationale were explained as follows:

> The setting for the project described in this report is Jackson County, Kansas, a northeastern rural area with a population of 10,342 in nine small towns. The Neighbors United (NU) Board, an outgrowth of MH 14888, served as the local sponsoring body for the project in the county. The NU board, representative of all adult age groups, was drawn from local civic and community organizations.
>
> The overall objective of the project research was to conceptualize indigenous helping activities in a rural Kansas county where no professional helping resources (i.e., psychiatrists, psy-

chologists, social workers) were available. The primary objective of the demonstration was to enhance and nurture indigenous helping efforts without changing or modifying those special or different qualities helpers bring to helping situations. Prior to project implementation, two groups of indigenous helpers were identified: natural helpers and paid counselors. (A natural helper is a person such as a grocer, neighbor, housewife, friend, and so on, to whom, because of the person's concern, interest, and "innate" understanding, people "naturally" turn for help. A paid counselor is a person who gives information and help in his area of specialty, for example, a banker, lawyer, minister, welfare worker, and so on.)

The specific aims of the project were fourfold:

1. To construct a conceptualization of indigenous helping relationships in a rural county and to test its adequacy and utility.

2. To describe the types of social problems encountered by different types of helpers classified according to the conceptualization referred to above.

3. To appraise the effectiveness of different types of helpers with different types of personal, family, group and/or community problems.

4. To explore, conceptualize and appraise ways in which counseling and helping interests can be mobilized and most effectively nurtured. This includes methods of developing and utilizing a team approach using a combination of indigenous and professional helpers. . . .

*Project Rationale.* The theoretical assumption underlying this research and demonstration project was that informal, unorganized networks of indigenous helping relationships exist in small towns and rural communities which cannot be duplicated and should not be supplanted by professional practice. Instead, these efforts should be nurtured and extended. Only when local efforts do not suffice should they be professionally supplemented. More specifically, this project was based on the following tenets:

1. Neighbors and friends on a voluntary basis give help to each other that cannot be duplicated by professional mental health counselors.

2. Local counselors, such as ministers, lawyers, educators, public assistance workers, county extension personnel, public health nurses, bankers and others who, because of their occupations give counseling services, make contributions that cannot be duplicated by professional mental health counselors.

> 3. Community mental health is strengthened by the maximum use of skills, abilities and potentials of neighbors, friends and local counselors. This applies both to persons who are receiving the counseling services and those who are rendering them. . . .
>
> Although the investigators believed the natural helper shared similar attributes or characteristics with the paraprofessional and the volunteer, he was also thought to be different. Unlike either of these helper classifications, the natural helper is not trained nor does he serve under any organized auspices. Additionally, unlike the paraprofessional, the natural helper is not paid for the services he renders. His helping efforts are, therefore, informal, unpaid, unorganized, and untrained. . . .
>
> A major assumption of the natural helper research was that those special qualities the helper brought to the helping situation would be in danger of change or modification if helpers were trained or organized. Further, the investigators strongly believed that frequently the resolution of a difficult problem or situation was to be found in the interaction of the helper and the helped rather than always through the expertise of the professional.
>
> The investigators had observed the natural helping phenomenon in both their professional and personal lives, but there was little concrete data to support their speculations. Unanswered were such questions as: Who is the natural helper? How does he help? Are the ways that he helps significantly different from the ways paid counselors help? Whom does he help? What are his attitudes toward the people whom he helps? What types of problems are encountered by the natural helper? In strengthening and maintaining the special qualities of the natural helper, how can the professional work most effectively with him? What is the nature of the natural helper–professional relationship? . . .
>
> In summary, then, these and other questions stimulated the investigators to explore the helping processes of natural and paid helpers in a rural area for purposes of conceptualizing indigenous helping activities.[2]

The first phase of the project was devoted to locating and interviewing natural helpers and counselors; the second involved observing and, when necessary, supporting their activities; the third included evaluating and reporting.

Natural helpers, it was found, dealt with twice as many different problems as paid counselors, and the problems that both groups dealt with were generally emotional ones. Both frequently encountered physical illness, marital difficulties, and bizarre behavior.

> Although none of the paid counselors were affiliated with school systems, this group had many contacts regarding school problems (14.3 percent) compared to natural helpers (3 percent). Infrequently, natural helpers were involved with problems of retardation, financial difficulties, mental illness, arguments between relatives, problems of youth which included drugs and difficulties with opposite sex, and loneliness of old people (3 percent each). Problems infrequently dealt with by paid counselors were: divorce, alcoholism, suicide, mental illness, illegitimacy, death, conflict of youth with parents and unemployment (3.6 percent each). Paid counselors (7.1 percent) were consulted more often regarding legal difficulties than were natural helpers (1.5 percent). . . .
>
> Regardless of their job or profession, people (that is, paid helpers when questioned) related experiences of successful encounters with natural helpers. Voiced were such comments as, "Why, it's just something you always have known about, but felt you could not prove," or "I use people like that all the time. I just never call them natural helpers." Others reported the project brought attention to and made more visible the role of the natural helper. As one man stated, "You feel you've just documented a hunch." The paid counselors were optimistic regarding the importance and potential of natural helpers. The philosophy underlying the project was confirmed by these groups. They expressed their belief that any attempts to organize, educate, or pay natural helpers would alter the intrinsic value of their helping activities.[3]

Project personnel viewed themselves as extensions of the skills and abilities of the natural helpers. At first the natural helpers frequently sought advice on how to deal with a situation, asked the professional staff to take charge of the problem, or, in some instances, requested that staff evaluate how the natural neighbor had dealt with the problem.

> It was difficult for staff to refrain from responding to these kinds of requests since traditionally such requests have been within the purview of professional activity. However, with few exceptions, project personnel managed to maintain the focus of increasing and extending helper confidence. . . .

> Evidence of increased helper confidence can be most clearly illustrated by recounting some typical examples. On one occasion, a staff member responded to a rather urgent call from a natural helper who was working with a neighboring family. Forty-five minutes and thirty miles later, the staff member was seated in the helper's home listening to an account of the helper's intervention with the family. At appropriate times the staff member supported the helper's actions. Preparing to leave, the staff member was somewhat puzzled since there did not appear to be an overwhelming crisis confronting the helper. The situation was clarified when the helper confided, "I didn't really need your help with this problem. I know I did a good job of handling it on my own. It's just that now I don't have much chance to visit with you any more." [4]

The project experience bore out the hypotheses. One finding may be of major importance in further research in this sensitive and newly discovered field. It is of particular interest in light of the discussion in Chapter 1 regarding the existence and the functions of natural networks and the characteristics of their central figures. This finding relates to mutuality.

> The content analysis of helper interviews revealed an unexpected finding of this study which identified "mutuality" as a critical variable that may differentiate the help-giving relationship of the natural helper from that of the paid counselor. The interview guide for this project was not specifically designed to elicit responses reflecting mutuality in the natural helper-helpee relationship. Had an answer been sought to the question, "How do you, as friends and neighbors, help each other?" rather than "How do you help other people?" the evidence regarding the presence of mutuality undoubtedly would be far stronger. Despite the fact that the former question was not asked, approximately thirty percent of the interviews with natural helpers indicated that mutuality is not merely one aspect of the helping relationship but does, indeed, provide the broad framework for meaningful help-giving and receiving. . . . Mutuality, then, in the natural helper-helpee relationship is not simply a matter of returning "tit for tat," as in reciprocal exchanges, but implies a depth relationship based upon doing, feeling and sharing with one another. . . .
>
> A major theme in mutuality, which recurred, may be described as the kind of help one gives and receives through sharing common conditions, problems and experiences. . . .[5]

In their conclusion, the directors summarized their view as follows:

> The demonstration confirmed that mutuality is a distinguishing characteristic of the natural helper-helpee relationship. Experientially, mutuality appears to contain such dimensions as acceptance, spontaneity, availability, follow-up, outreach, willingness to receive as well as give help, commonality of experience, and equality of status. These factors also appear to permeate the ways natural helpers help.[6]

## *THE GATEKEEPER PROJECT*

In contrast to the Kansas mental health project, which sought out natural helping people in a rural area where organized helping agencies were nonexistent, the "gatekeeper" project reported by Robinson was carried out in three urban districts of Philadelphia: "an elegant upper-class white neighborhood; a sprawling lower middle-class white neighborhood not far away, peopled largely by Italian and Polish working families; and an adjacent black ghetto neighborhood."[7] The project seems to support the idea that there are individuals who are in occupations bringing them in close contact with people and who use these contacts in helping ways. It was based on the hypothesis held by Dr. John A. Snyder, the psychologist who directed the program, that

> . . . many people in the community are not impressed with the mental-health-giving ability of the professionals. Most people in distress prefer to take their emotional problems to someone in the neighborhood whom they know and trust.[8]

Who these people—called gatekeepers—were and how they functioned were the first questions that the project attempted to answer.

> There were men and women of most ages, races, religions, and occupations. They included beauticians, barbers, bartenders, teachers, corner druggists, grocers, delicatessen proprietors, doctors, policemen, school-crossing guards, ministers, priests, and even two nuns.
>
> The survey shattered one of the most cherished illusions in community mental health work. It had long been believed that the vast majority of people—68 percent as indicated by earlier studies—looked first to their clergyman or family physician

for advice on emotional problems. The researchers discovered that this wasn't true. In the lower economic groups, a mere 15 percent turn to clergymen or physicians. The figure is barely 24 percent in the upper economic classes.[9]

Having identified the gatekeepers, the project staff wrote and asked them whether they would be willing to take part in a mental health training program without pay. More than two hundred agreed to do so and were offered regular seminars on crisis intervention and marital counseling taught by members of the project team. Team members also provided consultation and support to individual gatekeepers through frequent interviews. The hospital made special arrangements to provide the gatekeepers with emergency backup services so that they could get advice on how to deal with serious psychiatric problems at any time of the day or the night or could refer patients directly to the emergency room. However, the project report cites examples that, in the main, involve domestic crises and preventive intervention. Among them are these:

> . . . the quiet 55-year-old owner of a small family grocery store on 2nd street recalls a young wife who complained that her truck-driver husband was running around with other women. The husband admitted it. "Rocky," he said, "my wife, she nags, nags, nags. I can't stand it any more."
>
> [The grocer] never pulls punches. "Maybe if you stop nagging at him so much," he told the wife, "your husband would start staying home nights."
>
> She took his advice, and the couple began to get along much better.
>
> . . .
>
> Alcoholism and drug addiction are continual problems. "Tony, Joe was drunk all weekend again," a gray-haired woman says to a barber-gatekeeper. "What am I going to do? You did so much when you talked to him before. Please, Tony, will you talk to him again?"
>
> The barber persuaded Joe to go on the wagon once more.
>
> . . .
>
> One of the most dedicated gatekeepers in the project was the leader of a teenage street gang, a 16-year-old boy. . . . Eddie, the son of a Philadelphia fireman, was an instinctive gatekeeper. All the boys and girls in his neighborhood brought

him their troubles. They kept his family's telephone busy until 1:30 in the morning.

"I'm a listener," Eddie explained. "Lots of times, on my block, I hear kids talking and talking. I look around and I'm the only one listening." [10]

Eddie is of special interest in light of the high school counseling project described in Chapter 5. It seems to us that individuals like Eddie could probably be identified in a specific high school even more easily than in a large urban area. If they were encouraged to do more of what they were already doing—which might well be listening rather than tutoring or acting as a resource for referral—then a more effective, self-perpetuating program might develop at much less cost in time and money.

In another example Robinson illustrates an aspect of "gatekeeping" sometimes overlooked. He tells about a mother who sought help for her pregnant 16-year-old daughter from a friend who was a drugstore proprietor—a man from whom almost everyone in the neighborhood asked advice. The proprietor reassured the mother that the family would not be disgraced, talked with the girl about the alternatives, and maintained contact with the family throughout the girl's pregnancy, helping her to make decisions about adoption and marriage from his lifelong knowledge of the neighborhood and of all the persons involved.[11] This kind of relationship based on intimate long-term acquaintance and carried on over time is rarely possible for professionals.

Still another example from this project raises interesting issues. A beautician reported to the team psychiatrist that one of her customers was discouraged because her affair with an older married man was not going well. The psychiatrist urged the beautician to ask the woman if she ever thought of "ending her life." When the beautician agreed to do so after some protest, the customer admitted to constant suicidal thoughts, and while she was under the dryer the beautician arranged to have her admitted to the hospital at once.[12]

Although the result of the intervention was good in this instance—probably because of the psychiatrist's good judgment about both the beautician and the customer—the action taken would seem to be a dangerous precedent for services that did not have a strong professional support system. Even more crucial is the possibility that other beauticians who are not natural gatekeepers might, upon hearing about such a case, consider it their duty to take similar action with negative results. Overreliance on occupation is illustrated by the fact that—because of the publicity about beauticians and bartenders who are natural neighbors or gatekeepers—several state and city-wide programs have undertaken to train all beauticians and bartenders to be intervenors in emotional problems. This approach ignores the subtle relationships in a helping network and the awareness built up over time as to who the good helpers are. Training all persons in a particular occupation, without regard to their individual abilities and inclinations, would be counterproductive both for the intervenors and the public. This might confirm the impression, already widely held, that it is dangerous for anyone but a highly trained professional to counsel those who need help.

## *A NETWORK-CLAN ON A RESERVATION*

The professional in "network therapy," according to Attneave, is neither a catalyst nor a social director but rather an orchestral director. This is a useful image, although she readily admits that "good conductors do more than beat out the time and set limits for individual solos or subgroup harmonies but specifying what they do in objective terms is difficult." [13] She describes experiences with existing clan networks of American Indians as a means of clarifying "some of the essential elements of the therapist's role" and tells how one such network on a reservation was mobilized on behalf of an Indian child.

Attneave's discussion of the characteristics of the network-clan is interesting in itself and also as an example of the kind of study needed for other natural networks if intervention is to succeed. Attneave points out that, although her own intervention was "facilitated by a heritage of Indian descent, these skills can be acquired by non-Indians who are genuinely interested and concerned." She believes that the same factors operate in urban networks, but they are often masked because it is assumed that a common culture exists. The background of a child referred to her was described as follows:

> The case of Maria was a direct referral after the court's Child Protective Agencies had intervened. An Indian mother was

> charged with child abuse and a six-year-old girl had been placed in a foster home before the therapist was peremptorily summoned [from a mental health clinic] to the task of making clinical evaluations, and "doing therapy." . . .
>
> The mother, who was from a deprived nonnurturing family of another tribe in another State, had borne this girl before her present marriage and had left her at age 3 months to be raised by the maternal grandmother. After acquiring sufficient education to become both socially and geographically mobile, this woman had entered into a marriage with a man from a different tribe and was raising four more children successfully. Into this household was thrust a previously rejected child symbolizing a repressed and rejected past.[14]

That rejected child was Maria. When she had reached school age, her situation had come to the notice of officials who ordered that she be removed from her grandmother's home and returned to her mother, Mrs. T, with little time to prepare either her or the new family for the change.

Attneave notes that this situation might have been viewed in a number of conventional ways and that action might have been taken when local officials removed Maria from the home as a battered child and placed her in a foster home. A social activist might have attacked the insensitivity of white officialdom and taken the case to court. Traditional case therapy might have been started with Maria and family therapy with those in the home, which included at the time of this referral four younger children and the stepfather's 80-year-old father.

In fact, the therapist's first visits focused on understanding the home and its influences on Maria, and these visits revealed that Maria could not meet the expectations there after growing up in the neglectful care of an alcoholic grandmother. It did not surprise the therapist to learn that Maria had not fitted into the family, had been disruptive, and had served as a constant reminder to her mother about her own rather shaky status in the new family and the larger network-clan.

It was the presence of this clan that changed the therapist's position from that of a family therapist to "orchestral director."

> This network-clan had been concerned about the problem of Maria and was scheduled to convene that weekend to consider it. A non-Indian therapist might not have been invited to attend, or might even have attempted to convene a similar meeting else-

where. In this instance, a recognition of intertribal kinship as well as professional concern about Maria and her family brought about the invitation for the therapist to attend the meeting, and the therapeutic arena shifted.

*Induction into the Network-Clan.* The first meeting was almost like moving into a marathon session since it lasted from sundown to sundown and involved, all told, about fifty people. After a hearty and fortifying supper, the key family members, about twenty adults, sat in a ceremonial meeting all night. Others cared for children, visited and prepared a regular and a ritual breakfast as well as the mid-day feast.

During this first meeting there were three types of change accomplished. One, the therapist was inducted into the network-clan. It was now possible to define the professional role as that of helping them solve problems in their own context, not of imposing outside solutions. Being a participant gave the therapist maneuvering power as a part of the network as well as providing a link to the outside world. Two, there was a better definition of the problem as details were shared. Three, the helplessness which everyone in the network felt was non-destructively expressed.

At this stage, it was possible to shift the attitudinal balance from one that piled on shame and guilt, with ostracizing behavior, to one of shared problem solving. But good will alone is not enough, and much work continued in related areas.

*Network Intervention—"Indian-Style" Therapy* Another absent ghost had haunted the parental household, that of the grandmother who raised Maria and her mother. Following the generally expected principle that talking about her might lead to insight and regeneration, the topic was introduced during the continued family sessions.

It is tempting to describe the frustrations experienced by a traditionally trained psychotherapist interacting with the Indian culture. When one's whole learning is oriented around discursive discussion, insight development, and verbal tools, it is disconcerting, to say the least, to seek for toeholds in a situation where they are not the model avenue of communication. Perhaps this exchange about the grandmother will give a sample:

Therapist: "It might help us understand if we knew more about your mother—."

Mrs. T reacts with a startled glance, immediately her eyes lowered to her lap, and a faint blush. . . . Grandfather directs a piercing look at therapist and then stares out the window. Mr. T sugars his coffee and shifts in his chair, checking visually the group around the table. . . . Therapist sits like a bump on a log . . . as do all the others.

Mr. T picks up his cup, sighs and says, "Well, it might—." More silence, but it feels less tense.

At this point, a 4- and 3-year-old tumble into the room excited and everyone's attention is shifted to their immediate needs.

As this confusion simmers down, the family turns their attention to practical immediate problems. School is to begin shortly and they feel Maria should be at home to begin locally. A weekend before school opens is also time for another meeting and they wish to use it to celebrate Maria's birthday along with that of one of the younger siblings, according to their custom. Permission for the visit as well as the therapist's participation is arranged. An hour or so later, as time to leave arrived, one of the older men asked the therapist abruptly, "You think it might help if we knew more about the grandmother?" The only possible response is to count silently to ten, echo aloud the father's earlier, "Yes, I think it might," and finish putting on one's coat while listening to the familiar "um-gh" in response.[15]

The therapist carried out the plan and brought Maria to her family some weeks later, having helped her plan her reentry into the family. To the therapist's surprise and Maria's delight, her grandmother was there with the others to greet her. "The network, mulling over the therapist's remark, had stretched its links across two states and brought the absent grandmother to spend two weeks!"[16]

During the next twenty-four hours, there were rituals of receiving Maria into the clan, ceremonies that included her mother, stepfather, and grandmother. In the afternoon Maria played with the other children of the tribe, and their elders went about accustomed tasks.

Grandfather T, the eldest member of the network-clan, stopped beside the therapist and watched the same scene. After a few minutes he observed "Hum—a good idea to get to know that grandmother. . . ." Then with a piercing glance and the suspicion of a twinkle he gathered himself up to walk off. Turning he raised an arm that embraced the group below in a majestic sweeping gesture—"That is much better than a lot of noisy talk."[17]

The therapist's contacts did not end with this dramatic resolution of the problem. She accepted her professional responsibility for mediating with the court and other agencies, and kept in touch with Maria and her family, undertaking to understand and resolve the problems of clan acceptance faced by Maria's mother. She was able, too, to help with some of the problems the younger children presented as a consequence of Maria's reentry into their home.

> The dual roles of supporting appropriate role behavior and catalyzing and clarifying interactions in the various sub-systems were interspersed with periods that permitted ventilation of feelings and instruction in child care and normal development. Holding all this together in context was the sharing with the network-clan joys, sorrows, tasks, and satisfactions. In this setting, Network Therapy becomes a variant of participant observation that might be termed "participant intervention."
>
> At the end of fifteen months, this family had survived several other crises without disintegration. Both mother and daughter were functioning well socially and intrapsychically. The network-clan remained intact and consisted chiefly of the grandfather, wife, husband of this family, 5 paternal aunts and their families, together with about 8 or 10 other families of men designated as uncles or nephews in the Indian way.
>
> At the latest word, this network-clan had coped with arrangements for the guardianship and protection of another patient—a handicapped youth whose parents had died. Their plan and efficiency have saved the white community the cost of institutional care, and the youth from developing a full blown psychosis. In between such meetings for therapeutic purposes, the network-clan has celebrated birthdays, coped with the disruptions of death, the drafting of young men, and welcomed home Vietnam veterans.[18]

## DAY CARE NEIGHBOR SERVICE

It may seem easier to work with a network as well established as the one Attneave described that has a visible kinship boundary than to do so with the kind that social workers more often encounter. In our discussions about the potential of work with natural networks we often encountered the argument that this approach might indeed work with a well-defined, operating network, but that these hardly exist anywhere any more and certainly are lacking in deteriorated, low-income, highly transient urban areas. Although our deep convictions were to the contrary, the day care project undertaken by Watson did not set out to counter skepticism.[19] Rather, it aimed to explore the potential of natural networks as a means of preventing abuse and neglect.

One unexpected finding during the first years of the Day Care Neighbor Service was that Day Care Neighbors knew about the children who were not well cared for by their own parents and were anxious to help remedy the situation. In several instances, Day Care Neighbors—with minimal support from the social work consultants—had intervened in cases of serious neglect and abuse that were not known to professional agencies. Watson recognized that child welfare workers had long been concerned about their inability to identify cases of this kind and remedy the situation before they had become "so flagrant that the only alternative often caused further damage to children and their families." With the limited funds remaining in the last year of the Day Care Neighbor Service, Watson organized a demonstration project in cooperation with the public child welfare agency to

> explore the possibilities of the Day Care Neighbor Service model to increase and improve preventive and protective service. It was believed that it would be possible to identify neighborhoods in especial need of protective service, and that it would be feasible to recruit day care neighbors from these neighborhoods.[20]

To the prospective Day Care Neighbors—if they could be found—the objective of the project would be explained in terms of the help they were giving to their neighbors in any way, not merely in preventing the neglect of children.

A public welfare agency in a nearby community was interested in participating, and arrangements were made for Watson to carry out the usual Day Care Neighbor procedures for six months, keep the agency informed of her progress, and introduce a designated member of the agency staff who would carry on the program at the end of the six-month period.

The two women that the welfare agency staff named as key figures in the neighborhood—Mrs. York and Mrs. Cook—were also named by the many other people whom the consultant talked to in the neighborhood. Each of the women managed the trailer court in which she lived. They were often troublesome and demanding, and neither would have seemed a likely colleague without those advance recommendations.

> The York home was next door to the trailer court surrounded by a cyclone fence with signs warning visitors of the menacing dogs usually visibly guarding the front door. Safe entrance, according to Welfare staff, required one to knock on the side of the old two-story house until a family member came out and held off the dogs while the visitor came through the yard, up on the porch, and into the house. Once inside, the danger from the dogs subsided and the competition with the blaring TV, the healthy noise of the eight children, and the repetitive chatter of the myna bird began. . . .
>
> The Cooks lived in a two-bedroom mobile home located opposite the middle of the long pink apartment building. The dilapidated but colorful pick-up truck, used for transporting Mrs. Cook and her yard maintenance equipment by which she earned her living, was parked beside the trailer when she was at home. Before reaching her door, an approaching visitor would have been spotted and appraised by many tenants in the court. Sharp barks from her old black cocker spaniel let Mrs. Cook know of oncoming visitors and she often called out a welcoming "c'mon in" before knowing who was knocking at her door. Usually there were tenants sitting around her kitchen table drinking coffee, exchanging the latest bits of gossip in the court and discussing the state of the nation as it affected them. They seemed to melt away when a stranger appeared unless Mrs. Cook urged them to stay, which she sometimes did.
>
> Mrs. Cook tended to deny her own central position in the court despite the obvious fact that her kitchen was like Grand Central Station. She claimed that she rarely had time for "coffee klatching" with neighbors since she was out earning a living. However, when invited to become a Day Care Neighbor, Mrs. Cook readily made time available to meet with the consultant on a regular basis.

*Description of the Tenants in the Courts* Most of the tenants in both courts were known to one or more of the welfare, health, medical, and law enforcement services in the community. They tended to move frequently, sometimes from one of the courts

> to the other, and were often described by community services personnel as "hard core" cases. . . .
>
> Both courts had rental space for mobile homes and also offered low-cost housing, small tacky cabins in one and tiny motel-like apartments in the other. [The managers] were responsible for selection of tenants, collection of rent, distribution of mail, and management of the laundry facilities provided in each court. In addition to their official duties Mrs. Cook and Mrs. York provided a multitude of fringe benefits to their tenants: transportation to medical facilities, for groceries and surplus food, for welfare and job applications; advice about marital relationships, child care practices and provisions; resolution of neighborhood conflicts; information regarding community resources; tea and sympathy over small and large problems.[21]

Mrs. York, having herself known severe parental abuse, was sensitive to it in the trailer court. In one instance, she observed that the father of four young children brought home only small bags of food to the family. Through her own highly developed "casework" approach, she learned that the mother, married at 14 in a southern state, was afraid to let anyone know that both she and the children were severely undernourished and hungry and that her husband abused all of them when drinking. Brushing aside the wife's fears of what her husband would do if he found out, Mrs. York enlisted the help of the public welfare department and the police and finally had a number of face-to-face encounters with the husband that, more to the consultant's surprise than Mrs. York's, resulted in much better family relationships and certainly improved the physical conditions.

> One of the hazards of giving Mrs. York support and encouragement in her day care neighbor role was her tendency to build fantasies of herself as a kind of superwoman savior. Mrs. York's tendency to try and manipulate resources was her way of handling her fear of exploitation and rejection. The consultant provided anticipatory guidance to ward off disappointments, hold down Mrs. York's drive to over-extend herself, gain a reality-based perspective of community services.
>
> Mrs. Cook was less prone to aggrandizement of her day care neighbor role than Mrs. York. In fact, the consultant encouraged even more involvement by pointing out how important she was to her tenants. The consultant learned from Mrs. Cook's description of her past and current experiences that she was more adult

> than child oriented; she viewed herself as vulnerable to authoritarian figures, institutions and attitudes; though she denied her expertise she did observe and evaluate the quality of child care in her neighborhood; she knew about community services and used them appropriately. As Mrs. Cook told about her history, the consultant noticed that she was clearly more emotionally involved when describing her adolescence and young adulthood than her early childhood. And it was the young women in her court who were of prime interest and concern to her. Mrs. Cook seemed to get vicarious pleasure from her young tenants' narcissism and fast pace of living but their acting out of rebellion and violence terrified her, especially when it was directed against her.[22]

Mrs. Cook felt this conflict especially about one unmarried mother who partied most nights, leaving her baby alone or with the young man in the next-door apartment who was a mentally disturbed homosexual. Mrs. Cook was alternately distressed and angry about the baby's neglect and pleased at the wild escapades and fun the mother was having. She was torn between her conviction that she must report the situation to the welfare worker in charge of the case and her reluctance to turn the mother in. The consultant helped Mrs. Cook sort out her feelings so that she could take action to protect the baby and yet could withstand the storm of the mother's short-lived anger.

One of the consultant's objectives was to help the Day Care Neighbors see community agencies more as allies than adversaries. This was no small task since both women had had personal experiences that had prejudiced them against community institutions. At the same time, the consultant endeavored to interpret their helping potential to the welfare agency and to develop the relationship of colleagues which could best serve the tenants of the trailer courts.

A month before the six-month demonstration ended, the consultant introduced the agency staff member who had volunteered to carry on the consultative service to the Day Care Neighbors. Although the small stipend of $25 a month that had been paid to them could not be continued and both were always living on the edge of financial disaster, the Day Care Neighbors were not at all discouraged about continuing. They expressed regret about losing the consultant, but they were obviously pleased that the welfare agency considered their activities worth the investment of its time.

> Just after the new consultant began working with the day care neighbors the question of confidentiality arose. Mrs. Cook, especially, felt that her neighbors would interpret her talking with the consultant from welfare as a breach of loyalty and that this might interfere with her effectiveness in the court as well as with the consultant. The welfare consultant dealt with this on a reality basis, emphasizing that Mrs. Cook was free to say no more than she felt comfortable and could interpret her day care neighbor role to her tenants however she wished. Once the pressure was off and it was clear that she was not expected to be a "stool pigeon" Mrs. Cook relaxed and continued her role as she had done in the past.[23]

The project consultant helped the welfare agency consultant adjust to her new role, which was quite different from her usual one. The welfare worker remarked that, although she had previously accepted the concept of Day Care Neighbor Service, she did not become cognizant of the helping potential of Mrs. Cook and Mrs. York until she began to work with them as colleagues. She continued her contacts with both the neighbors and with the project staff until the agency's reorganization made this impossible.

As in so many preventive projects, evaluation of this project's success could only be done in subjective terms, given the limited time, resources, and methodology available. The impression coming out of this service confirmed the impressions of a number of projects cited in this book. There was a conviction that natural networks exist at levels that would otherwise be

> . . . out of the reach of professional social workers who are well aware of the serious problems existing there.
>
> The trailer court project was also a test of the concepts and methods developed in the Day Care Neighbor Service for social work consultation with natural networks. It demonstrated that natural neighbors could be found in even so transient and alienated a milieu as the trailer court, that they could be recruited as colleagues although they had had no previous experience with such a relationship, that they could greatly enhance professional understanding of the strengths and problems of their culture, and that they could make use of the relationship to

increase their tolerance of the behavior of the network members and thus augment their helpful interaction with them.[24]

The project also confirmed the belief that agencies having heavy official responsibilities could incorporate into their routine duties some consultation with natural neighbors. Doing so should help to offset the frustration that competent social workers often experience from the pressure of their daily work and their relatively negative contacts.

# Notes and References

1. Shirley L. Patterson and Esther E. Twente, "Utilization of Human Resources for Mental Health," Final Report (Lawrence, Kans.: University of Kansas School of Social Welfare, 1972). (Mimeographed.)
2. Ibid., pp. 1–7.
3. Ibid., p. 50.
4. Ibid., p. 62.
5. Ibid., p. 38.
6. Ibid., p. 69.
7. Don Robinson, "Gatekeeper," *Family Health,* 4 (April 1972), pp. 24, 72–74.
8. Ibid., p. 24.
9. Ibid., p. 24.
10. Ibid., p. 72.
11. Ibid., p. 72.
12. Ibid., p. 72
13. Carolyn L. Attneave, "Therapy in Tribal Settings and Urban Network Intervention," *Family Process,* 8 (September 1969), pp. 192–210.
14. Ibid., p. 197.
15. Ibid., pp. 199–200, 201.
16. Ibid., p. 201.
17. Ibid., p. 202.
18. Ibid., pp. 203–204.
19. Eunice L. Watson, "Trailer Court: A Day Care Neighbor Approach to Protective Service" (Portland, Ore.: Field Study of the Neighborhood Family Day Care System, 1972). (Mimeographed.)

20. Ibid., p. 4.
21. Ibid., pp. 16–19.
22. Ibid., p. 40.
23. Ibid., pp. 60–61.
24. Ibid., p. 65.

# part two

# How to Work with Natural Networks

# 7

# *Summary of Consultation Method*

The projects quoted in the preceding chapters made use of a variety of ways of observing and working with natural networks. We planned in advance to use mental health consultation in our project of day care service and did so, with some modifications. At this time consultation seems to be the method of choice in social work with natural systems.

Rapoport describes consultation as follows:

> It is conceived of as an activity which in essence is concerned with problem defining and problem solving. . . . It is characterized as an indirect service. . . . The purpose of consultation is to introduce change in some facet of the consultee system. . . . The more immediate goal . . . is to strengthen consultees in their designated professional role. . . . Consultation takes place through a transactional process in which help is given with work problems and in which some technical knowledge, relevant to the problem under examination, may be transmitted. The consultant carries a staff rather than a line function and thus has no administrative authority over the outcome of the work. His authority rests on his status as expert and on the administrative sanction which allows him to enter the consultee system. . . . Consultation, furthermore, is viewed as a time-limited, goal-oriented, and segment-focused transaction. . . . The consultation role may be assumed without any special preparation, but increasingly . . . more formal patterns of education will emerge to give substance and sophistication to this area of social work practice.[1]

A brief review of the method's history will help in considering how social workers may use it with central figures in natural systems.

As early as 1915, consultation with physicians and teachers was described as a necessary and important duty for social workers.[2] But it was not until the passage of social security legislation in the 1930s that the term consultant was used to designate social workers carrying the specific role. The first consultants were well-trained professionals affiliated with public funding bodies whose task was to help disbursing agencies meet the standards and deliver the services that would insure the continued eligibility of these agencies for grants in aid. In the past twenty years, as special funds for local projects became more available, consultants at the federal and state levels have also served as consultants to local agencies, assisting them to write proposals that would qualify them for such funds.[3] In theory, the consultants met the definition of the role since they had no direct responsibility for carrying on the daily work of the local agency. In practice, however, the consultants had some responsibility for the disbursement of the funds because of their recommendations to the parent disbursing agency, so that the essential confidential relationship did not really exist. Furthermore, the local agencies were not free to accept or reject the consultants' suggestions.

## *THREE LEVELS OF INTERVENTION*

Over the past twenty-five years the model developed by Caplan has increasingly influenced the consultation that social workers, psychologists, and psychiatrists in community mental health have provided to teachers, nurses, and other professionals.[4] According to Caplan, intervention in community mental health, as in public health in general, may be considered to occur at three levels: primary, secondary, and tertiary. The focus at the primary level is to prevent the occurrence of illness. Innoculations against disease, the passage and enforcement of pure food and drug laws, safety regulations, mental health education projects, and well-baby clinics are examples of health measures aimed at primary prevention. The thrust of secondary prevention is toward early recognition and prompt treatment at the onset of illness or accident to prevent serious *sequelae*. Readily available and financially accessible outpatient and inpatient diagnosis and treatment are examples of effective secondary prevention. At the tertiary level, the focus is on providing ongoing rehabilitation or similar services in an effort to prevent further deterioration or permanent crippling of those already impaired by illness. Most mental health and social welfare programs have been designed for intervention at the secondary and tertiary levels, because effective techniques for primary prevention are often lacking.

Shortly after World War II, leaders of the mental health movement realized that direct service—even at the secondary level of prevention—to all who needed it was not feasible. Primary prevention, while universally recognized as desirable, seemed even less attainable. They began to consider how to apply preventive health concepts to extend the reach of the relatively few trained individuals who might be expected to be available for service. Crisis intervention theory, which was being developed at the same time, also suggested new uses of mental health manpower. This theory holds that at a time of crisis an individual loses the ability to use his customary means of coping and becomes dependent on others. The resulting disequilibrium tends to last a relatively short period of time and then homeostasis will be reestablished, because individuals cannot long support the anxiety of crisis. The resolution of a crisis can lead either to increased coping skills or decreased ability to meet the next crisis. The outcome of crisis is intimately connected with the presence or absence of individuals who are immediately available to provide needed support at this crucial time.[5]

Although mental health professionals accepted the principles of crisis intervention and saw their potential for prevention, they realized that they were rarely able to put these principles into effect because they themselves were not close enough to those experiencing crisis to reach these people as quickly as was essential. Furthermore, even if individuals in crisis were willing and able to ask for help from a mental health facility, these facilities were rarely organized to respond as promptly as necessary. However, many other professional people were in daily contact with individuals in crisis, and these professionals could and often did intervene. It seemed feasible to back up such caretakers—nurses, teachers, physicians, ministers, and policemen—by providing consultation with mental health professionals. Thus, professional assistance with problems related to mental health could move toward a true community service that might insure intervention at all levels of prevention.

## MENTAL HEALTH CONSULTATION

Mental health consultation developed from these assumptions, and principles of practice that can be used for guidance have been formulated. A first step toward establishing a relationship for mental health consultation is directed toward the administrators of the organization with which the prospective consultee is associated. Since the consultee must voluntarily seek consultation, an invitation to the consultant by top administrators initiates the relationship. Admittedly, the consultant may make an effort to prompt the invitation but should not overstep the role. Furthermore, assurance that consultation is welcome must be renewed from time to time with the administrators.

Administrative sanction should not, however, become coercion. The mental health consultant probably will need to make sure that the prospective consultee is free to decide whether to seek consultation. The consultant is responsible for understanding the setting or learning enough about it quickly enough so that help proffered for problem-solving will be consonant with the possibilities open to the consultee.

Once the relationship between consultant and consultee has been initiated, the consultant may utilize a variety of treatment techniques to help solve the problem the consultee presents. Whether educational, collaborative, or therapeutic approaches are used, the consultant applies them always as a colleague, whose special skill is directed toward helping the consultee attain the competence aspired to in the chosen professional role. The consultant's objective is, in fact, a dual one: to make sure that those the consultee serves—students, patients, clients—are assisted toward their highest possible level of functioning and to help the consultee grow in the ability to deal with similar future problems unaided.

Attainment of these goals requires skill in rapidly diagnosing problems from the viewpoint of the client or the viewpoint of the consultee, and even from the perspective of the effect of the setting on the problems. Treatment can then be carried out at whatever level or combination of levels seems feasible.

Treatment through consultation does not involve therapy at a deep personal level. In fact, consultation related to any single problem is usually limited to three interviews or less to avoid initiating a treatment relationship, which would be contrary to the basic principles of relationships between colleagues. Furthermore, extended consultation on a single problem would rapidly create the kind of unmanageable caseload that mental health consultation aims to avoid. This is not to say that consultation terminates with the agency after three interviews. Rather, it is desirable for a consultant to be on call over a long period of time so that the confidence built by one successful consultation may power others between the same consultant and consultee or other consultant-consultee partners when new problems arise.

Consultation may be provided on work problems at every level including the administrative, the only limit being the consultant's evaluation of personal competence to carry out the request effectively. Each assignment for consultation resembles the professional model in general but has its own idiosyncracies. The consultant is responsible for eliciting the information needed to make a maximum contribution, and this information usually comes best from the consultee. At all times, the consultant must bear in mind the lack of authority over the consultee's performance, which means that the consultee is free to take the consultant's advice or leave it and may choose to ask for future help or not. In the practice of consultation it is this aspect of the consultant's role that is perhaps the most difficult to accept. It is this aspect also that makes the difference between the basic partnership of consultation and other relationships. Although, in some settings, certain consultants carry only consultative responsibilities, in general consultants also have other professional responsibilities, such as direct treatment. Thus, they must be clear at all times about which "hat" they are wearing so that they do not confuse one role with another.

Caplan's frame of reference for his model of consultation is the mental health clinic, where professionals are seen to have a legitimate concern about the mental health of the entire community. Hence there is a rationale for offering consultation to a variety of caretakers who deal in some way with the mental health of a population. Social workers also serve as consultants to caretakers in other systems, such as hospitals or courts, with more narrowly defined goals. In every setting, the goal is to assure that individuals—whether they are in crisis or face problems of other kinds—have ready access to effective preventive intervention from those who are in continuing contact with them.

# Notes and References

1. Lydia Rapoport, *Consultation in Social Work Practice* (New York: National Association of Social Work, 1963), pp. 18–19.
2. Richard C. Cabot, *Social Service and the Art of Healing*, "NASW Classic Series" (New York: Moffat Yard and Co., 1915; reprinted: Washington, D.C.: National Association of Social Workers, 1973).
3. Esther Spencer, *A Casebook of Consultation* (State of California, 1969).
4. Gerald Caplan, *Principles of Preventive Psychiatry* (New York: Basic Books, 1964).
5. Lydia Rapoport, "The State of Crisis: Some Theoretical Considerations," in Howard J. Parad, ed., *Crisis Intervention: Selected Readings* (New York: Family Service Association of America, 1965), pp. 22–31.

# 8

# Modifications in Techniques of Consultation with Natural Neighbors

We believe that consultation at every preventive level is well suited as a method for social work use with natural neighbors. By identifying central figures in helping networks and extending consultation to them, social workers can have an impact on the prevention of social dysfunction at all levels, especially the primary level. Through consultation, social workers can strengthen the neighbors' ability to be helpful to members of their networks. The central figures are uniquely situated to deal with crises and to prevent the development of more serious problems that require professional intervention. How does the theory of consultation apply in social work with natural neighbors? We will attempt to answer this question from our own relatively limited experience and that of persons who carried out some of the projects quoted in Part One. As techniques continue to be tested, practice will no doubt be refined.

## *DIFFERENCES IN STATUS*

In work with natural neighbors, most modifications of conventional consultation practice occur because natural neighbors differ in status from the usual professional consultees. The problems that concern natural neighbors cannot be said to arise from their work, even though many may have a defined work status, since their role as natural neighbors is apart from the job they are paid to do. Moreover, these natural neighbors cannot be expected to define problems and ask for help from a consultant. For the most part, they do not perceive themselves as dealing with problems, and they do not consider that they need problem-solving help from professionals.

Natural neighbors have a firm sense of their own identity, but, unlike conventional consultees, they do not have a title that indicates to the larger society what their function is. Because they lack this designation, they lack ties to each other and do not have the support and public recognition accorded professional consultees. Natural neighbors are not likely to see social work consultants as a resource since they probably have had little experience with social workers in any capacity, especially as consultants. These differences between natural neighbors and the usual consultees deserve mention, but in no way should they be regarded as bases for invidious comparison. In fact, natural neighbors make excellent partners in a consultant relationship. They have a great deal of specialized knowledge about their networks acquired through study that is no less serious because it is informal and independent. Most natural neighbors have taken advantage of information presented in mass media and other resources on subjects they know to be significant for members of their networks, and they feel a personal responsibility to update what they know. Even though their position is untitled, it is a firm one within their own network. They are all experts on their own network and have a sense of the interrelationships within their network as a whole as well as the situations of its individual members and its relationship to the larger community.

The self-image of these central figures as highly competent people to whom others turn makes it relatively easy for them to accept social workers as partners. Paradoxically, because they lack specific understanding and direct experience with the helping professions, they have fewer of the stereotypes that, in more conventional settings, sometimes interfere with establishing a firm relationship of consultation. It may well be that the natural neighbors will find it easier than the social work consultants do to move into the partnership of consultation. Some hindrances for the social work consultant have already been mentioned:

(1) the tendency to make the newly discovered role of the natural neighbor conform to an existing familiar one such as that of the paraprofessional, (2) the training syndrome, and (3) the absence of administrative structure that ordinarily introduces and legitimates the consultant to the consultee.

## PRIORITIES

Social workers may also be troubled by questions of the priority of needs. Almost every social work practitioner has seen evidence of the possible negative impact of professional settings in schools and hospitals, the conventional consultee institutions, for example, and feels that if the professionals who work there would change some of their practices, the preventive effect would be felt at every level. But little is known about the effect of positive natural networks except that they seem to be functioning well on their own. The question then arises: When so many people plainly need help and professional staff for providing it is so limited, should time and effort be given to working with a system that is apparently functioning well without professional intervention? The view that intervention should be directed chiefly toward serious problems is becoming less acceptable both to the profession and to the community. Social work is under increasing pressure to demonstrate the value of its services to large populations. The time seems to be at hand when exploring primary prevention is an imperative, not an alternative.

It is not surprising that even professionally trained consultants may hesitate to initiate a service with natural neighbors. In addition to the already mentioned ways of diverging from the familiar, such a service presents the problem of identifying those to whom consultation is to be offered—a first step that is indeed alien to other professional practice. The process of identification will be discussed more fully in another chapter.

Our experience and that of some other professionals who have developed alliances with natural networks suggests that it is often easier to enter these networks than to enter conventional settings of consultation. There is no overall hierarchical structure to be negotiated step by step, and there are fewer stereotypes and interdisciplinary rivalries to dispel. On the other hand, the consultant has no established institution to work with and does not even have a clear definition of what to look for when seeking natural neighbors. Consequently, consultants must be much more aggressive in entering a network than they are accustomed to being. Contrary to the social worker's usual task of dealing with persons who are finding it difficult to cope, the consultant's task is to seek out the very individuals about whom they have least professional knowledge—persons who are functioning well in their own lives and are interacting well with their peers.

Having identified these people, the consultants must offer them a relationship for which there is not yet a precedent, one that the natural neighbors do not expect and indeed may see as unnecessary or even undesirable. Nevertheless, once the relationship is established, its positive rewards far outstrip its negative aspects and, we think, may replenish the consultant's emotional resources to a greater degree than any other kind of consultative relationship can. Natural neighbors tend to be stable within their networks, which permits a relationship of mutual trust, insight, and continually expanding learning to develop for both partners over time. By gaining a better understanding of the role the natural neighbor plays and a greater appreciation of the skill with which it is performed, the consultant recognizes the presence of a strong ally in a difficult task. Having such an ally may help prevent the despair and frustration that is an occupational hazard of a profession continually being made aware of the imbalance between human need and available help.

## *STABILITY OF NATURAL NEIGHBORS*

The relative stability, independence, and uniqueness of natural neighbors leads to another apparent difference between consultation with them and with professionals. The consultant to teachers in a school or to professional staff in a public health department is likely to have a changing population of consultees as individuals come and go, even though there will always be a teacher in the sixth grade or a public health nurse in X district. Short-term consultative relationships with several individuals in a given setting are feasible in these conventional frameworks and have been shown to be a method of choice.[1] On the other hand, a helping network presumably has only one natural neighbor, who has a high degree of stability. If the neighbor terminates activity —because of a move out of the community, personal illness or loss of interest—replacement is questionable and how it might come about is doubtful. Much study is needed in this area. For the present, the recommended procedures are (1) to carry on consultation with natural neighbors over as long a period of time as it seems to be rewarding to both partners and (2) when necessary, to follow the same procedures in identifying a natural neighbor's successor that were undertaken initially.

Another easily overlooked dimension of the relationship distinguishes the partnership from one in more conventional settings; that is, this partnership can provide the consultant with a firsthand view of the interrelationships among network neighbors and the relationships, at every social and political level, between members and the larger community. It offers the consultant a participant-observer's view of the impact that social change and health and social services have on the recipients. Consultants are in a position to learn how services of every variety are viewed by their consumers, how they are used, what works, and what does not work. Consultants may thus become the only professionals in a given area who not only know what the problems are but how successfully they are being met. They have a chance to acquire a base of information for advocacy unrivalled even by the settlement house leaders, since these consultants are not confined to a close acquaintance with deprived neighborhoods but have the opportunity to develop partnerships at every level throughout the community. Work with some groups, such as the blue-collar middle class, is less familiar, but social work consultants may find that it is as important for primary prevention as work with clients and classes traditionally served.[2]

## *GOALS OF CONSULTATION*

The goals of consultation with natural neighbors are similar to those of consultation with professionals, but there are some variations and additions. The major objective remains the same: helping the consultees solve problems in their practice and increase their ability to do so unassisted in the future. The range of problems that the consultees deal with may, however, be broader than that of the professionals, and problems may be more diffuse. Consultants may need to rely more heavily on their role as partners seeking answers than that of experts offering solutions. In conventional consultation settings, consultants confine their efforts to helping consultees improve problem-solving within their assigned position. In working with natural neighbors, consultees have an additional goal—to encourage natural neighbors to enlarge their circle of influence and at the same time improve the quality of their intervention at every level. This does not mean that consultants will attempt to convert natural neighbors into paraprofessionals or leaders for social change, but only that they will help natural neighbors include individuals who are within their customary sphere of influence but are not personally known to them. "Neighboring" once referred to all people living within a given geographic area, not merely friends or those who took on an active neighborly role. In some neighborhoods today it is often considered a breach of good manners—or sometimes unsafe—to introduce oneself to strangers or otherwise approach them. Natural neighbors usually know a great deal about the strangers as well as the friends and acquaintances within their orbit, but their approach is often restricted by taboos about "minding your own business." Hence they may fail to offer help they realize is needed. If the potential of each person in the area is to be fulfilled, consultants will wish to encourage natural neighbors to widen their circle of influence to include all those they see as needing their assistance.

# Notes and References

1. Gerald Caplan, *The Theory and Practice of Mental Health Consultation* (New York: Basic Books, 1970).
2. Robert Coles, *The Middle Americans: Proud and Uncertain* (Boston: Little, Brown & Co., 1971).

# 9

# *Finding Natural Neighbors*

In giving specific suggestions about organizing a natural neighbor service, we have tried to be practical. We do not mean to imply that the only way the service should or could be given is to follow these suggestions. We have assumed that an existing social agency would undertake the service, but this is not a prerequisite. There is limitless room for experimenting with, amending, and adjusting the model presented.

The most crucial work of developing a natural neighbor service goes on during the period of planning and decision-making that precedes actual practice. It begins customarily when the agency's administrative staff realizes that the agency is underserving a population for which it has responsibility. Some traditional means of improving existing service delivery will probably be considered first, but this may not prove feasible in terms of time and money. Hopefully, one of the next alternatives will be an exploration to determine whether there are new ways to deliver services that might reach the population at risk within the limits of whatever funding may be available. Establishing an experimental system of network consultation might be the alternative chosen.

A firm commitment to the natural neighbor concept will be needed. To operate this service, a staff member who is presently functioning at top capacity in a direct service role will have to be freed to become a consultant to a much less definable and less visible population. At first, this may appear to curtail rather than increase service, and it may actually do so until the relationships with natural neighbors are well established. Eventually, through consultation with natural neighbors, the agency may expect to serve more clients more effectively than it did before introducing the system. It may also be able to function in a preventive fashion for many more persons who might have become clients if the service had not helped to keep problems from developing.

The director of the agency must be prepared to support the effort until it begins to pay off. Some staff members may find the goal of this service nebulous and may consider that moving away from familiar service delivery techniques is so threatening that they will disqualify themselves as candidates for the new position of consultant to natural networks. Potentially successful candidates are likely to be staff members who quickly grasp the possibilities and volunteer enthusiastically. However, more than enthusiasm is essential, since the consultant's job demands a high degree of professional training and experience, preferably in direct service and in consultation with professionals.

The consultant should be chosen as soon as possible after the agency decides to explore the inauguration of a service. Whether or not a service results, further investigation should be the consultant's responsibility because the investigative process may lead to contacts with members of the natural system who may become partners in the service. Even a decision not to attempt the service could be useful to a consultant since the investigative experience could become a basis for subsequent explorations.

The suggestions that follow grew out of our experience with helping networks in urban neighborhoods. As the wide range of examples cited in the foregoing chapters indicates, such a program could have quite a different base. Networks exist, for example, in offices and factories, in scattered rural villages and settlements, and among migratory populations. Seemingly, when consultation is to be established with a neighborhood network, the only necessary condition for successful consultation is that the natural neighbor have ongoing contact with other members of the network. Of course distance and other factors would influence the frequency and type of contact between the consultant and the natural neighbor, but general procedures could be adapted to a variety of situations.

## *FIRST STEP IN EXPLORATION*

Although the consultant will want to begin by determining the geographic location of the population at risk, the first step in the exploration that looks toward establishing the service—contrary to expectations—will not require going into the field. Useful data are, as a rule, readily available from a variety of sources. Suppose, for example, the population at risk involves patients returning to the community from a hospital or other institution for the mentally ill or the mentally retarded. The patients' addresses at the time of commitment and release can be obtained from the institution, from public and private committing agencies, and from individuals who have resumed responsibility for the patients upon their return to the community. The locations of the persons to be served may then be plotted on a map.

The next step is "backtracking"—which means seeking to discover whether natural neighbors may be involved at present, or might be recruited to involve themselves, with the individuals at risk. The paths of individuals at risk who have made successful or unsuccessful adjustments are traced into the past from the present. A trail of failure is more likely to be visible than one of success. For example, a good deal of information is usually recorded about the mental patient who had to go back to the hospital a number of times and who never made a successful community adjustment. Certain facts may suggest what caused the recidivism. The question to be asked is not who was to blame but who might have intervened. Social workers may at first glance have blamed themselves or other professional colleagues, but an objective review often shows that the absence of some trusted person who might have given support to the family or the individual accounted for the failure.

Looking into the successes is likely to yield more information about natural networks than looking into the failures. This search begins with identifying ex-patients who have adjusted well to community living, even though many had presenting problems similar to the problems of those who failed. Names of such individuals may not be easily obtained from the agencies involved; troublesome patients tend to be better known, but records of the well-adjusted exist. It may be possible to find out enough about them to develop hypotheses as to why they succeeded. It may well be found that a supportive individual contributed to the success by intervening directly with the patient or by supporting and encouraging the family or others in the patient's environment.

Another way to discover natural neighbors is described in the Trailer Court project (Chapter 6), in which the initial step was asking professionals who were in touch with an entire disadvantaged population to describe individuals known to take an interest in others. When these individuals started to cooperate with the professionals, the agency at first considered them troublesome because they constantly demanded service on behalf of others. It became obvious, however, that their demands reflected a genuine interest and a willingness to become personally involved.

## *GEOGRAPHIC PLOTTING*

When all the information gathered about the community, the population at risk, and the natural neighbors is plotted on a map, the agency and the consultant can probably see whether geographic clustering exists that will justify inaugurating a service that is essentially neighborhood based. If the target population is thinly scattered over a wide area, attempts to serve it through a natural neighbor network probably could not succeed.

If the situation warrants it, an agency may organize a natural neighbor network with less than the amount of information ideally desired. The Day Care Neighbor Service that antedated the Trailer Court project had little data on the population the project wished to serve, but some community center staff had the impression that the community badly needed day care service. In such a situation, a study of census figures may help determine in what neighborhoods the population might be expected to reside. In the case of the Day Care Neighbor Service, we looked for neighborhoods where there were married women working, a high proportion of young families, and many single elderly persons who we had thought (quite erroneously) would be serving as family day care givers.

While carrying on the geographic plotting, the consultant will also be collecting information from colleagues within and outside the agency. Initially, these colleagues are likely to express ignorance of any natural networks in the population at risk. This should not be surprising since the target population was chosen because it was underserved. However, when interviewing skills are used and the area of interest is approached indirectly, a colleague may recall that indeed a client has discussed a relative or neighbor who recently returned to the community from an institution and then may proceed to describe the situation in detail. Looked at from the new perspective of what the agency's exploration has revealed about neighborhood networks, the consultant's own practice may prove to be a surprisingly good source of a good deal of information about the community relationships of the population at risk.

## *RECONNOITERING THE NEIGHBORHOOD*

Having decided on a neighborhood that appears to have both individuals who need service and some who seem to be natural neighbors, the consultant will wish to learn as much as possible about that neighborhood in terms of history, social and ethnic makeup, and so on. Then, and not before, is there readiness to physically reconnoiter the neighborhood. It should be kept in mind that people in the neighborhood will note the consultant's presence, even in an urban setting outwardly unresponsive and preoccupied with its own affairs.

We are strongly of the opinion that a formal survey of the neighborhood is contraindicated, although an inexperienced consultant might feel more secure in carrying out this time-honored procedure than in acting more passively as an observer. Information collected in such a survey tends to be unreliable—especially if the questionnaire or interview form was designed to be quickly coded and thus may not have recorded important verbal and nonverbal communications. Many respondents view surveys as an invasion of their privacy, and formal ones may interfere with future productive contacts. Also, with market surveys having become prevalent today at every socioeconomic level, respondents tend to suspect that the interview will end in a sales pitch—a fear that carries over into subsequent contacts too. Furthermore, in disadvantaged or minority neighborhoods, so many surveys are likely to have been conducted without bringing about improved services, that residents may project past frustrations onto the present interviewer.

Perhaps the most significant reason for not conducting a formal survey is that the more effective the natural neighbor is in maintaining the network, the less that neighbor or members of the network recognize that the neighbor is using problem-solving skills. The mental health project in Kansas (Chapter 6) suggests that questions about resources for problem-solving do not elicit useful responses about natural networks. This does not mean that the consultant avoids asking questions in the neighborhood chosen. On the contrary, such questions as these will be well-formulated before arrival at the scene: Who in the neighborhood is in touch with the group needing help? Who seems most concerned for the welfare of the individuals in this group? Who provides some service for them? What do the residents think about the service?

The consultant will also want to find out what the invisible boundaries of the neighborhood are. Ways to discover the location of these boundaries include first-hand observation, reading local newspapers, and noting community advertisements in store windows, on bulletin boards, in laundromats, or in markets. The consultant will carry on informal interviews with pharmacists, personnel of food markets, school secretaries and janitors, the leaders of formal and informal organizations, church personnel and parishioners, and others. Just drifting about the neighborhood, having coffee or a beer, or standing in supermarket check-out lines will fortify impressions. If the preparatory historical work has been done well, an observant and attentive consultant will soon be able to delineate the boundaries of the neighborhood. No doubt, repeated references will have been made to certain individuals who can provide the information sought and who are actual caregivers to the population inquired about.

Besides noting certain names, the consultant will listen with discrimination, because what is said about these people will be one of the best guides to their position in the network. For example, it may be said that a particular apartment-house manager "just loves old people" and prefers to have them rather than families with children in the building. This may mean that this manager is a person who likes to look after the needs of elderly tenants and bring them together for mutual help, or it may mean that he sees the elderly as the least destructive and troublesome of tenants and the least demanding of a manager's time and energy. Obviously the manager interested in meeting needs would more likely be a natural neighbor. It is our experience that residents of the neighborhood understand what the consultant is looking for even if this is not explained too clearly. They may well mention spontaneously and accurately a person who "knows all about that around here."

At this point, when the consultant has already invested a good deal of time and effort without actually "starting to work," it will be tempting to hurry into actual recruitment just to get started. However, it is advisable to restrain this impulse, in order to assure the best possible selection. Terminating a relationship with an ill-chosen natural neighbor is unquestionably more difficult than tolerating the anxiety of further deliberation.

## *INTERVIEWS WITH CANDIDATES*

When several possible natural neighbors have been identified, the consultant makes an informal personal ranking of the candidates and in turn asks for an appointment with each one as a recommended expert in the community. The interviews, then, will focus on the candidates' general knowledge and their opinions about the neighborhood without being specific about the purpose of talking with them. This approach is much more familiar to anthropologists than to social workers, who are trained to be receptive to offers of help but not to initiate them and to confine interviews to confidential discussions of one client's immediate concern rather than encourage a free-ranging, gossipy description of all kinds of personal situations of many people. Such chatty interviews, however, will be the main avenue of intervention when the service develops, and at this initial meeting the consultant can practice the technique as well as identify the central figures who may become consultative partners in the service.

Any hesitation and doubt about the service in general may well be dispelled after a few such interviews. The best prospects are persons accustomed to requests for help of all kinds. They are likely to respond easily and openly to inquiries, having themselves made an informal but remarkably penetrating estimate of the consultant's trustworthiness. As in the exploratory conversations throughout the neighborhood, the consultant will not need to spell out the precise projected plan or list professional credentials at length. Genuine interest in the people who are of concern to the candidate—those with current identifiable problems and those who can be mobilized or assisted before serious problems develop—will be the best references.

The interview, if conducted on the prospect's "turf" as it should be, is likely to be subject to many interruptions which themselves may offer clues for evaluating the prospect. The phone will ring, neighbors will drop by. Are others asking the candidate for help? Help of what sort? How does the candidate respond? Natural neighbors tend to take it for granted that a request for help takes precedence over the interview, and they expect the consultant to agree.

The patent content of the interview will be the target population and what the natural neighbor can tell the consultant about it. The consultant will no doubt use both direct and indirect questions, will encourage the prospect to talk freely, and will of course avoid interjecting too many personal views, particularly if they are not in line with those of the natural neighbor. After all, the aim is to learn, not teach; and the hope is to act as a partner, not a critic. Probably the prospect will also inquire into the views and even the personal life of the consultant. This curiosity may be accepted for what it is—the conventional first step in building a friendly relationship—and the consultant should respond to it in an equally informal, open fashion. This is not to say that the consultant should provide a full life history but only that this kind of question should not be rejected as it might be in a therapeutic encounter. The response could be like that to any casual acquaintance met elsewhere.

The consultant may consider this a long, drawn-out, and indirect procedure—and it is—just as the preliminaries to establishing a productive professional relationship under more familiar auspices are likely to be. In spite of personal impatience to get started and the expressed or unexpressed pressure sensed from the agency, the consultant will do well not to recruit a colleague in consultation at this initial interview but to wait until after reviewing all interviews planned. Through this delay, serious consideration can be given to two questions: Are the effects of the network positive or negative? Is the central figure motivated by the kind of mutuality of relationship that provides the energy for truly helping networks?

In attempting to find answers to the first question, the consultant will wish to discover whether the network encourages its members to maintain socially unacceptable behavior or to make and continue positive contacts with each other and with the larger community. Some bartenders, for example, might well be central figures in negative networks, in contrast to Peter, the bartender described by Dumont in Chapter 3. Similarly, some of the other SRO residents might be contrasted to the dominant leaders described by Shapiro (also in Chapter 3). Since we have focused our efforts in developing techniques of consultation with the central figures functioning in a socially positive direction, we have no advice on ways that might be successful in reversing the direction of negative networks. It is our impression, however, that this is an extremely difficult task and one that needs to be considered for the future. We recommend, therefore, at the present state of the art, that the consultant not go beyond relationship with networks which have a positive influence.

In our own projects we developed criteria that would help us identify central figures in day care systems and make predictions about their success which we could then evaluate.[1] These criteria included easily measurable attributes such as the Day Care Neighbor's age, economic circumstances, family makeup, and other objective factors that vary with the population served. The one criterion that we believe is of primary importance and that pertains to all situations is less objective and requires the judgment of an experienced professional. We call this *freedom from drain,* which indicates that the individuals are sure about the strength of their own emotional and physical resources and enter into relationships with others out of mature concern.

Earlier chapters have stressed the conviction that helping relationships expressed mutuality and brought rewards and satisfaction. Freedom from drain has no correlation with the age, sex, education, or income of the natural neighbor. The consultant will depend on professional skill to make the final judgment on the basis of information collected directly and indirectly, observation of nonverbal behavior, and the many other small signals.

### RECRUITING A PARTNER

Having decided which prospect is most likely to be a central figure free of drain in a positive network, the consultant is ready to recruit this person as a partner. Even when full time is devoted to the consultative role, it would be a mistake to recruit more than two natural neighbors at a time. During the first few weeks the work with this type of service is time-consuming and does not allow for developing a partnership with more than two persons. Furthermore, if this is indeed a new role, other customary professional activities should still be carried on for the sake of the consultant's own mental health during the period of anxiety when a new kind of helping relationship is being initiated.

## Notes and References

1. Arthur C. Emlen and Eunice L. Watson, *Matchmaking in Neighborhood Day Care* (Corvallis, Ore.: DCE Books, 1971).

# 10

# Establishing a Consultation Service

The preliminaries to initiating a service may have seemed intolerably drawn out to the consultant and to the agency administrator who is under constant internal and external pressure to improve services. It is a protracted process, but so is entry into other more conventional consultation settings in which the consultant must lay the groundwork with agency administrators and then wait for the consultee's invitation. Once neighborhood systems and their central figures are identified, the steps leading to a functional relationship of consultation are relatively easy, and they then proceed more quickly than similar moves in more conventional settings. There is of course no need to obtain administrative sanctions since each natural neighbor functions independently. Although the neighbor may also be part of some hierarchy, that aspect of life does not have a bearing on prospective relationships with the consultant.

As has been mentioned, the consultant may safely count on a natural neighbor's friendly interest in any person or plan that offers the prospect of improved services to network members. However, it would be unrealistic to expect that this central figure of a network will understand, at a first recruitment interview, the concept of consultation, which may be new to the consultant as well. Nevertheless, it is important at the outset to state the general outlines of the contract for consultation, which can then be referred to, refined, and restated throughout the relationship, just as in other professional encounters.

Natural neighbors tend to have an extremely modest view

of their activities, and many insist that they are not "doing anything." Yet the relationship of consultation is based on the fact that they do a great deal; therefore, it is important for the consultant to tell the prospective consultees just why they have been asked to join in a partnership. The consultant may mention what was personally observed about the consultee's place in the network and in the regard of its members, what the consultee does with the people and for them directly, and what is done to facilitate productive arrangements between them. The hoped-for outcome of the consultation can then be realistically if not exhaustively described. At the first interview the consultant will probably have heard of the natural neighbor's concern about people seen or heard about in the neighborhood but not known personally. Problems of these individuals can then be used to illustrate how the natural neighbor may wish to use the consultant's support to enlarge the neighbor's present scope of activity.

The consultant will try to bring these things to the relationship: professional training in understanding human behavior as people interact with the environment, knowledge of community-wide resources, and willingness to talk over whatever the natural neighbor wants to discuss about the network. Besides explaining these proposed contributions, the consultant will express interest in learning about the natural network from the natural neighbor and commend the neighbor's ability to cope with its needs. In this commendation the consultant's own skills and professional roles need not be denigrated, although it may be pointed out that from the consultant's position, it is not possible to reach the people whom the natural neighbor has easy and frequent access to.

The consultant will continually stress potential mutual benefits from a partnership, will describe the mutual concern that those within the network or on its fringes will be as well served as possible, may point out that the role of consultant to natural neighbors is still in the developmental stage, and will indicate that both partners will have much to learn from each other.

## *FUTURE MEETINGS OF PARTNERS*

Hopefully, the recruitment interview will end with the natural neighbor's acceptance of the relationship and with a clearly defined program of future meetings when both consultant and consultee will have opportunities to get to know each other better, which they need to do as a basis for developing an ongoing partnership. The consultant will take the initiative in setting up the pattern of these meetings and suggesting interviews at weekly or biweekly intervals for the next month or two. The proposed schedule should be convenient for the natural neighbor, and interviews should be held wherever the natural neighbor is most comfortable—probably at home or in his work setting. The consultant should be quite explicit about expectations for these meetings and point out that their objectives are not to inquire into the success or failure of the helping activities in the network or to urge the natural neighbor to become a paraprofessional. A natural neighbor may readily think of both possibilities because nonprofessionals have frequently encountered them in the past.

It should also be pointed out that, when the introductory interviews are over and the partners know each other better, the consultant will be available to the natural neighbor on call, either by interviews arranged at agreed intervals (monthly seems about right) or irregularly, as the natural neighbor chooses. If there are qualifying conditions about the program—for example, the collection of data for research—they should be clearly described to the natural neighbor at the time of recruitment.

## *ANXIETIES ABOUT THE RELATIONSHIP*

Neither partner is likely to understand fully the range and ramifications of the partnership when these initial explanations are made at the recruitment interview. The consultant may well have second thoughts about the wisdom of the choice of the natural neighbor and doubts about the possibilities of success, as well as the usual anxieties common to consultation practice. And the consultant's anxiety may be heightened by that of the natural neighbor who, shortly after cheerfully and enthusiastically agreeing to become a partner, is likely to withdraw as a candidate because of qualms about being well suited to the task. No matter how carefully it has been explained in advance that the natural neighbor will not be asked to assume more responsibility than desired, this seems so unlikely a proposition that most recruits will either forget that they heard it or discount it as not to be believed. The natural neighbor may also question being chosen for the role by a social worker, since social workers are known to be in touch with the disadvantaged and emotionally disturbed, not with the healthy and well functioning members of the community.

The natural neighbor may also begin to feel uneasy about lack of formal educational qualifications and training in contrast to the professional consultant. There may be worry too about possible community criticism, in terms of being seen as a gossip within the natural network, or even a spy for the professional. The natural neighbor may not necessarily express these uncertainties verbally. They may not even be conscious thoughts. The consultant is likely to become aware of the concerns through a phone call from the natural neighbor, regretting inability to continue in the relationship because working hours or tasks or status have changed or because a spouse or relative or friend disapproved. At this point, the consultant will do well to review briefly with the hesitant partner what has been said about maintaining the natural neighbor in a role already being played, accept the neighbor's anxiety, and present a confident expectation of the continued relationship. It was our experience that, although we almost always received such an anxious phone call between our first and second visits, when we returned for the second visit as planned no more was said about these doubts. They were evidently superficial uncertainties compared with the deeper, more fully developed wish to continue to improve and extend the role of natural neighbor.

One aspect of these initial interviews may threaten the continuation of the partnership because of its impact on the consultant. As previously noted, natural neighbors consider the demands of their networks more important than the consultant's visits. They are likely to give their work or their family responsibilities the same precedence over the visits. Thus it is not unusual for natural neighbors to postpone scheduled interviews early in the partnership or simply be unavailable when the consultant calls. The consultant must not evaluate this behavior in conventional clinical treatment terms. Rather, it should be accepted as illustrating the informal *ad hoc* character of most relationships in natural networks. The interview should then be rescheduled, and the natural neighbor's prerogative to set priorities should be gracefully accepted. Such an attitude not only will help the consultant avoid erroneous conclusions but will show the natural neighbor that what has been said about the consultant's adjusting to the natural neighbor's convenience is true. The consultant should, at all costs, resist any impulse toward formally rescheduling interviews at the office or emphasizing them unduly by telephoned or written reminders.

There is another kind of impact on the consultant that should be considered and provided for in establishing the service: the impact of consultation per se. Consultation is always a lonely job, and the consultant is always once removed from any primary source of evaluation—a situation that, in itself, is anxiety-producing. Added to this, there is often in the consultant's mind the same feeling about consultation that natural neighbors have about their helping activities within their network—the feeling that a consultant is not "doing anything." The sense of separation and the sense of nonaccomplishment are even more acute in consultation with natural neighbors than in traditional settings. In a school or in a health service, for instance, comments by other professionals may give some indirect support, or a change in the rate of referrals may indicate achievement.

In planning and developing a consultative service involving natural networks, then, a system of supports should be built in, so that the consultant to the natural neighbors has a supportive consultant in the parent agency who will become familiar with the undertaking and back up the work when appropriate. If an agency is conducting several projects to test the feasibility and value of the natural neighbor type of service, it will be helpful—especially in the early stages of the development of such services—for the consultants of the various projects to meet together regularly to exchange experiences and techniques.

It is probably inevitable that natural neighbors will respond more readily to the general mandates of a success-oriented society than to the consultant's assurance that neighbors should maintain their own role and style. Predictably, at an early interview, central figures will present to the consultant their concern about how they should begin to let people know they would like to make the many contacts they assume to be expected of them. They may also express, directly or indirectly, their anxiety about the consultant's judging the quality of the services already being provided. The consultant will be well advised to accept these concerns without much comment and then focus attention on hearing about the present system for disseminating information in the community. Do housewives talk things over at coffee hours in each other's homes? On the telephone? Do workers discuss personal problems in the lunchroom of the plant? Do people stand around at the corner store and talk to each other? Or do they talk to the store's employees? Singly or in a group? Do they find out what is going on beyond the neighborhood from the radio on the way to work? From TV at home? From city-wide newspapers? From community newspapers? From house organs at their plants? Discussing such questions will serve to restore the partnership balance between the consultant and natural neighbor, since it helps identify avenues through which the natural neighbor ordinarily gives and receives news—avenues that may now be used to reach persons just outside the usual network.

Once some of the avenues for reaching people are recognized, the natural neighbor is likely to wonder what to say and how to say it. There can, of course, be no single answer to this problem. It will depend on the target population to be informed, on the kind of service neighbor and network are engaged in, and even more, on the natural neighbor's individual preferences. In the Day Care Neighbor Service, for example, many different ways to communicate were used—word-of-mouth, advertisements in community and plant newspapers, notices on an apartment house bulletin board, announcements at a bridge club and a PTA meeting.

## *EXTENSION OF THE NATURAL NEIGHBOR'S SERVICE*

In the discussions, the consultant will make every effort to turn the natural neighbor's thinking back to familiar, habitual ways of functioning informally and away from the imitation of formal techniques. Once equilibrium is restored by renewed confidence in familiar ways of work, the natural neighbor will probably proceed readily and independently toward the first steps in widening the existing circle of influence. These steps, however, may lead toward another unsettling development.

Having realized that they have a helping role of some consequence and interest, natural neighbors will probably wish to demonstrate to themselves and to the consultant that they function in the way they are expected to. They will therefore assume that, as soon as they make it known more widely that they are available, they will be besieged by requests for help. It will seem ironical that the natural neighbors who, a few weeks earlier, were concerned that their expanded role would be too time-consuming or otherwise undesirable are now anxious because their helping activities are not any more time-consuming than what they had long been doing almost unconsciously. It is important for the consultant to assure and reassure them that even a 50 percent rise in their interventive activities would probably not involve more than five or six additional interviews a week and that, with their skill and experience in carrying on such interviews, they might hardly notice they were extending their reach. It should be reiterated throughout the life of the service that the consultant does not judge the natural neighbors merely by the number of arrangements and contacts that they make; they are free to do as much or as little as they have ever done.

This is especially difficult for the consultant to do, because the number of increased contacts is one of the criteria for judging the success of the partnership. No doubt the consultant is under some constraint to produce evidence that this type of intervention is worthwhile; nevertheless, the consultant must guard against unconsciously putting pressure on the natural neighbor to fulfill these demands. One way to deal with this problem would be to avoid record-keeping entirely so that there could be no standard against which the natural neighbor's performance might be measured. However, this is unrealistic.

## *RECORD-KEEPING BY THE NATURAL NEIGHBOR*

No matter how difficult and alien record-keeping may be to the way the natural neighbor has functioned, it is an essential part of the service. Whether or not services should be judged in cost-effective terms, they will be so judged. At present, inaugurating a new kind of service is doomed from the outset if the service cannot be presented eventually in cost-effective terms, to some degree at least.

Besides providing essential evidence of accomplishment for the sake of accountability, maintaining adequate records offers other benefits to the consultant, the consultee, and the community. Since natural neighbors tend to minimize what they are accomplishing in the network, some of them who are housewives go to work outside the home for the measurable rewards, even though they would prefer to maintain their home-centered role. It is therefore useful for these natural neighbors to be able to see how many contacts they have made, recall their relative success and failure, and look at the increase over time that hopefully will come from their widened scope of activities.

The consultant also benefits from the "counting game" that record-keeping makes possible, and has the added benefit of becoming more familiar with the network through the records kept. Thus, eventually, the consultant may be able to map contacts in a way that is interesting and illuminating to professionals and nonprofessionals alike and that may provide a base for future community planning and service delivery.

Yet this difficulty remains: record-keeping is alien to the role of the natural neighbor, and requiring it violates a principle of the service, which holds that nothing should be asked of natural neighbors that is not already part of their usual functioning. It was our experience that none of the natural neighbors in the Day Care Neighbor Service, regardless of their educational background, spontaneously kept records of their contacts as we had asked them to do. We had supplied especially attractive and practical notebooks, but none of them kept a running record of contacts. A few jotted down arrangements made, and some noted requests from both givers and users of day care.

Initially, we were critical and, in some instances, importunate about their failure. On the taped records of our interviews, the tone of voice we heard ourselves use was more like that of a supervisor to a careless worker than that of a colleague collaborating on a joint enterprise. This strongly suggested that we needed to change our approach on record-keeping and find a way to facilitate it without friction. Our own solution was to continue to suggest that the day care neighbors make notes for themselves, written or otherwise, and that at the end of each month we would go over their notes and comments with them, and as we reviewed them we would record them with the help of the tape recorder. Then in our office, we could convert the information into the format required for formal data collection. This proved to be acceptable, and we found that the recorded interviews provided increasing and illuminating insights into the entire network. The records suggested questions that we asked about intercommunications, and the natural neighbors were often stimulated to describe neighborhood customs and systems that we might not otherwise have heard about. We knew that we were still retrieving only a portion of the record of the day care neighbor's contacts, but we felt we had no choice but to accept this limitation if we were to maintain the relationship on which the entire service rested. Whether this would be the case in other natural neighbor situations is unknown, but we believe that the projects described in Part One offer some evidence to indicate that it is typical.

It goes without saying that the consultant must also keep adequate records of work with the natural neighbors. This is an important element of the service, without which any significant evaluation of the undertaking is impossible. Records of the consultant and of the natural neighbors would of course be correlated in presenting periodic reports of the service to the agency.

## *A NEW KIND OF RELATIONSHIP FOR NATURAL NEIGHBORS*

Natural neighbors, being especially perceptive people, will note from the outset that the relationship offered by the social worker is unlike others they have known. To define the relationship—although not necessarily verbally—and to explore the possibility of establishing it are major undertakings of the entry period. One point the consultant may make to encourage the colleague relationship is to tell the natural neighbor that professional social work practice presents the same kind of difficulties that the natural neighbor describes. For example, in the boarding house project (Chapter 3), it was useful to let the operators know that the mental health team, too, had recognized the problems of dealing with heavily medicated individuals.

When consultants are clear about their own role, they should not have undue difficulty in establishing the consultative relationship with natural neighbors because their own body of experience prepares them to do this in other fields of practice. However, natural neighbors may find it harder to adjust to a relationship with a consultant. These central figures of a network may have had no previous opportunity for a close association with a person who is neither relative, friend, nor acquaintance and who neither needs help nor is providing it in any familiar manner. Any previous contacts that the natural neighbors have had with social workers probably took place under conventional circumstances and in conventional settings. It is not surprising then that natural neighbors, at the first few interviews, will try out the relationship with the consultant, seeking consciously or unconsciously to discover what the partnership is, what it will ask of them, and what they may gain from it. This is one reason why natural neighbors who, in early interviews, have quite casually discussed their families and their personal lives, as they might with a chance acquaintance, now return to the subject in more intimate detail. In part, this reflects the general view that people in the helping professions expect to hear personal history and, in part, the view that social workers see personal details as a subject of interest, as physicians presumably see ill health. An appropriate reaction may be difficult for the consultant. Neither the therapeutic role that ordinarily would lead to encouraging personal confidences nor the role of a casual acquaintance should be assumed. The most appropriate stance to assume will be that of two professional acquaintances who are exchanging *curriculum vitae* before they move into a true partnership.

If the consultee has been well chosen and no cataclysmic events have taken place since the choice was made, there will be little need for the consultant to guard against becoming involved in the natural neighbor's personal problems. However, this may occur. If a direct appeal for personal help is made, this should be dealt with as any such appeal would be in a more conventional consultative setting. The consultant should suggest a resource that could help with the problem and might offer to make necessary arrangements, but should remain firmly uncommitted to the helping role. There is a need to be sensitive to the difference between a real cry for help and the natural neighbor's assumption that the expected relationship is the conventional one of client and helper.

How can the consultant further the establishment of a consultative relationship and move away from the client-helper type of relationship that the natural neighbor may envision? The most obvious way is to generalize from the natural neighbor's personal concerns to the prevalence of similar problems in the network. From there, it is not difficult to move toward an interest in the natural neighbor's way of meeting such problems successfully. This approach restores balance to the relationship, because it clarifies for the natural neighbor and for the consultant the neighbor's role as a resourceful expert.

Another device that should prove useful throughout the relationship is for the consultant to ask the natural neighbor's opinion about techniques for managing members of the target population who have already come to the agency for help. What can be expected of the natural network in regard to a particular individual, perhaps a mental patient? How does the network view such patients? Would it be feasible to organize a natural neighbor service elsewhere in the city? Such questions should be honest. At the same time, the natural neighbor should clearly recognize that specific action in carrying out the services in question is not being asked for; rather, advice is to be given in much the same way as the consultant gives it for the natural network.

## *BEGINNING OF THE PARTNERSHIP*

When the consultant considers that a partnership relationship has begun, it will be suggested that interviews be spaced at longer intervals or arranged at the request of the natural neighbors. As in all other professional relationships, the time required to establish a firm relationship varies, and professional judgment must determine when this has been accomplished. There are usually some indications that it has been. The most obvious one will be the natural neighbor's returning to the confident tone of the recruitment interviews and telling—not asking—about the events in the network. The natural neighbor will describe these events and what was done about them, without anxiously asking for the consultant's opinion about the problems and their handling. The consultant will be able to give a professional opinion without deprecatory phrases about personal inadequacy to judge an unfamiliar system. The natural neighbor will freely agree or disagree with the consultant's comments and opinions and will no longer preface responses with remarks about his relative lack of education on which to base them. Certain rituals will be established and observed at each interview with regard to seating arrangements and refreshments. (Recalling preferences about cream and sugar is a nice indicator of partnership.) There may be "family jokes" based on incidents that occurred at earlier sessions or have been recounted from the network.

The consultant will have personal indicators too that will show whether or not a partnership has begun: looking forward to the interview without anxiety about the new role, losing track of interview time and discovering that the 50-minute schedule is no longer the controlling factor, noting situations in other agency practice that resemble those heard of in the network and interpreting them in the style of the natural neighbor rather than according to the professional stereotype, and possibly telling colleagues enthusiastically about the skills of the natural neighbor and the benefits of the natural network.

Perhaps the best indicator that a relationship has begun and that interviews need no longer be scheduled is that neither partner is eager to reduce the number of their contacts. However, this may also be taken as a sign of a beginning of personal interdependence that would not be useful if it were to develop. To prevent growing interdependence, the consultant need not hesitate to express regret at the prospect of less time together while stressing continued interest in maintaining contact with the natural neighbor and acquiring further details about the natural network.

It is important to convey to the natural neighbor that the consultant will be glad to be called "just to talk," to be told what is going on even though there is nothing that the natural neighbor considers enormously important or that presents a problem to be gone over together. Here, again, if a plan for data collection is necessary, it should be clearly explained and the routine discussed. The collection of data makes it logical for the consultant to maintain some kind of regular visiting relationship.

# 11

# Maintaining the Relationship

The point when the first phase of the relationship between the consultant and natural neighbors is completed is a crucial one for the success of the service. The consultant has invested considerable time and attention in inaugurating the service which, if efforts have been successful, is now reflecting an increase in the number and quality of the services rendered by the natural neighbors. Agency administrators may note this success and may well interpret it to mean that there is no further need for ongoing contact and that the scarce professional time devoted to the consultation can now be directed toward the agency's customary work or toward the development of other natural networks.

Even the consultant may believe that it is not necessary to maintain more than a data collection contact with the natural neighbors. New insights into the way they operate may have led to so great a respect for their skill that it seems there is nothing further a consultant can offer them. Natural neighbors may or may not accept the consultant's invitation to telephone, and the scheduled interviews still taking place may return to the polite chitchat of the first ones, confirming the impression that the natural neighbors really have no further interest in continuing a consultative relationship. The literature on consultation in the field of mental health will not be helpful because it advocates limiting contacts with any individual consultee while maintaining them with the consultee's agency. This does not apply because the consultee has no agency, but it may well confirm the consultant's belief that termination would be appropriate.

## *ALTERNATIVES IN MAINTAINING RELATIONSHIPS*

If working with several natural neighbors, the consultant may decide to start group meetings of all of them, instead of terminating relationships completely. This would of course reduce the number of meetings that would otherwise have to be arranged. We tend to believe, for a number of reasons, that group meetings are not a useful way to further the effective functioning of natural neighbors. For one thing, when a successful relationship is established, each natural neighbor comes to view the consultant as a friend and a partner. It would be disconcerting for any natural neighbor to discover that the consultant has the same relationship with a number of central figures of other networks. Such a situation could generate a variety of interpersonal problems that would not further the essential tasks of the partners.

Also, group meetings may become a kind of show-and-tell time in which each natural neighbor describes how problems are handled in a particular network, inviting comparison from others. The comparisons tend to become defensive and are, in themselves, not useful. It is axiomatic that no two networks are the same, nor do any two natural neighbors approach them similarly, and it is just because of that difference that the consultative projects were organized.

If group meetings are used to impart information, they then become training meetings, which are another form of put-down for the natural neighbors, or else they are used to transmit "housekeeping" information that could easily have been sent through the mails. Still another hazard of group meetings is that they put natural neighbors in the position of agency staff, and we do not believe that this offers any advantage. It is sometimes suggested that natural neighbors would enjoy meeting with each other socially. However, if well chosen, all the natural neighbors have a lively social life of their own and, should they wish to meet with each other, they can arrange to do so. It may also be noted that natural neighbors are protective of their networks. They are unlikely to talk about them with others who may well know some of the members, because they feel that this would put them in the position of being malicious gossips.

If, at this point, instead of organizing group meetings, consultants review their own feelings about the situation, they may discover that they are uncertain about their future role with the natural neighbors and that this uncertainty presents one reason why they are easily persuaded that the relationship could be terminated. The natural neighbors too may be wondering what more is expected of them. They may be somewhat anxious and defensive about their functioning, so that they do not welcome the consultant's visits as openly as they did at first. It might be said that, within a small social system, both partners are suffering from a dilemma described as a major cause of anxiety in society as a whole—the absence of guidelines for behavior or a lack of feedback from the environment that permits individuals to judge themselves against certain societal norms as members of society.[1] The natural neighbors, having been made conscious of their role and the possibilities of its expansion, now look to the consultant to learn more about what heretofore had largely been an unconscious functioning. The consultant, also exploring a new role, needs feedback about its effectiveness since there is little or no contact with the ultimate consumer of the service who usually provides this kind of report. Perhaps the proof that a successful partnership has been established between a social worker and a natural neighbor is the anxiety that both partners feel at this time about their contribution to it.

Rather than terminate the partnership or convert it into a different kind of relationship, the consultant should make every effort to maintain it, whether or not its cost effectiveness can be demonstrated at the moment. The responsibility to maintain the partnership and to assure that, according to professional standards, the relationship is productive for both partners remains with the consultant. This may involve taking the initiative a little longer in maintaining contact, until the natural neighbor begins to take over this function himself.

This interim period is not likely to be long. The natural neighbor will quickly readjust, begin to become more independent again, and use the consultant freely and productively. One factor that will contribute to a continued partnership will be the natural neighbor's increasing awareness of problems in the network. Frustrations familiar to social workers may be experienced since, with greater awareness of the problems other people face, more problems seem to be uncovered, ever harder to solve. In many instances, there may not be a solution to a problem; rather, there will be need for mutual support in the face of an obviously painful and destructive situation, for which no remedy is to be found.

Much of what the neighbors do is similar to what social workers do and is directed at the secondary and tertiary levels of prevention. However, the social worker will try not to lose sight of the primary preventive thrust of the service by focusing too intently on these more familiar activities and thus implicitly rewarding them. The natural neighbor will be encouraged to report on the innumerable small ways of maintaining the positive functioning of the network as well as on major problems and crises. Of interest, for example, are the trips to the hospital and the store for the ill and the elderly, the birthday parties planned and carried out, the child-rearing advice and substitute care given, and the marital and premarital counseling. By giving attention to reports of these relationships and services, the consultant conveys belief in their importance and promotes the idea of enlarging the circle of influence.

## *EFFECTS OF PERSONAL ATTITUDES AND PREJUDICES*

Personal attitudes and prejudices will at times inhibit the work of natural neighbors, just as they interfere with agency work. The consultant will consider it a personal responsibility to help the natural neighbor modify these attitudes and prejudices so that the goals of the service may be achieved more fully. As in all consultation, this effort will be undertaken by discussing the work problem and avoiding confrontation or trying to give insight, which would be contrary to a relationship between partners.

Central figures are likely to have strong opinions about agencies that deliver service. In the Day Care Neighbor Service, for example, the neighbor who was herself on welfare often urged working mothers to give up their jobs and stay home with their very young children. She pointed out that although the welfare allowance was small, it was regular and the workers do "all they can for you." On the other hand, the Day Care Neighbor from the top of the hill offered help to keep mothers employed and independent, because she believed that otherwise the taxpayer's burden would become intolerable. The day care consultant helped both these neighbors view conditions in a less personal light and give advice according to the individual situations of the mothers involved. An unexpected dividend from the consultant's efforts disclosed a possible long-range outcome. At a hearing on welfare legislation, the Day Care Neighbor from the hilltop voluntarily testified in favor of increasing welfare payments; she also advocated this view—quite new to her—in her private social activities, such as bridge clubs. She even defended unmarried mothers, who heretofore she felt should be blamed if not sterilized, because they had children they could not support. It was impossible to measure objectively the impact of this Day Care Neighbor's increased understanding and insight, but the consultant counted the outcome an excellent investment of professional time and effort since this neighbor was a member of a social group that influenced social policy in the community.

## *THE CONSULTANT'S UNDERSTANDING OF SERVICE DELIVERY*

The consultant will learn from the natural neighbor what is and what is not effective in present delivery systems of social agencies. This is illustrated in the SRO project (Chapter 3) in which one leader was well aware that the hospital was unwilling to accept certain categories of patients and devised successful ways to circumvent the obstacles. This might have shown the consultant ways to influence the hierarchy toward desirable change.

Contact with the central figures can give the consultant the kind of continued story that can rarely be followed from the agency base. The central figure describes what went on before the client applied for agency help and what follows its provision, and the consultant is able in some instances to be a partner in efforts that may either obviate agency intervention or increase its long-range effects. Throughout, the partnership will provide mutual support, the "I am not alone" strength and confidence that is perhaps the most potent force in improving individual and community functioning. In practical terms, it may become clear that, because of the natural neighbor networks, agency caseloads may be diminishing or that clients come to the agency better prepared to use its services. In addition to the consultant directly involved, other agency staff members may begin to use the central figure's skills in bringing together people in need and people who can fulfill the needs. When agency colleagues use these skills appropriately, they may well find that the agency will provide better service and that, at the same time, caseloads will decrease. The consultant's enthusiasm about discovering the resource of natural systems may also stimulate other staff members to wish to experiment with similar systems.

From the outset, a major objective of the service has been to encourage central figures to enlarge their circle. In a successful partnership, the central figure will begin to reach out to individuals previously unknown in the network, both through personal efforts and through referral from others, chiefly staff members from various community agencies. It will be the consultant's responsibility to refer agencies directly to the central figure, perhaps briefly explaining the role and certainly emphasizing that the central figure is competent in that role and can maintain the same kind of confidentiality as professionals, although using a different kind of problem-solving technique.

## *DURATION OF PARTNERSHIP*

How long the partnership between a social worker and a central figure should be maintained and what the problems may be in terminating it can only be discussed theoretically. To date, such partnerships have been delimited by being part of research projects that were arbitrarily concluded at the specified time. The role of a natural neighbor may be a lifelong one, or natural neighbors may relinquish the role for another one. For example, a home-centered woman may go to work, or an industrial worker may retire or take a job in another community. Individuals subject to many personal pressures may possibly become central figures late in life as they become more free of drain.

At the present stage in developing collaboration with natural networks, we believe it is important not to assume that the role of natural neighbor is a lifelong one. This assumption might lead to the practice, quite prevalent in foster care, of expecting a long-term commitment by the natural neighbor and gearing the program to this, when perhaps it may be more realistic to look toward continuous recruitment and renewal. Here, as everywhere, the partnership will indicate how the program will develop, and the consultant will follow the lead as the central figure decides whether to continue or terminate the role.

It is quite possible that the turnover of consultants will be greater than that of central figures, and because the partnership has been a dynamic one, the problems of separation when it ends may be expected to be acute for both partners. The consultant should prepare the central figure well in advance for the change and offer anticipatory guidance about the feelings that may be involved, perhaps illustrating the point by telling about personal reactions. When possible, the consultant's replacement should also be given anticipatory guidance about the central figure's probable reluctance to accept a new consultant. Our brief experience suggests that natural neighbors may express their sense of loss by deciding to change their life situation, go to work, assume extra responsibilities, or take on another program that they believe will preclude continuing contact with any consultant. When prepared for this reaction, the consultant can help resolve it in a way that will be satisfying to the natural neighbor and that will reduce the negative influence from the changeover to a minimum. The consultant will no doubt deal with personal conflicts of separation by recourse to the support system that has been developed within the agency.

The consultant's records of the service can be especially significant when partners are separating or the agency is terminating the service. It will be helpful for the consultant to be able to look back over an experience with a natural neighbor, note how the service has changed, and hopefully, see how much and in what areas it has grown. If the service has not expanded, a backward look—as in all recording—may help improve the techniques for a future undertaking. In our own project, we tape-recorded interviews with designated natural neighbors over time that gave a verbatim account of certain approaches, clearly showing their success or failure. We believe that this was an extremely useful educational tool for us, but it is difficult to say whether it would fit into other projects. When the interviews are not tape-recorded, it becomes doubly important for the consultant to keep as full a record as possible of their content and of personal opinions in regard to what happened in the course of them. Time should be budgeted for such recording since, without it, the project will have little material on which an evaluation can be based.

# Notes and References

1. Gerald Caplan, *Support Systems and Community Health* (New York: Behavioral Publications, 1974).

# Postscript

We have tried to plot a course that will lead others to discover an important resource and explore it further—which, in turn, will lead to new and better ways of providing service. All the foregoing pages attest to our enthusiasm about the possibilities that consultation with natural networks open up and to our hope that it will be widely used in the future.

It would, however, be irresponsible to close without once more drawing attention to the possible hazards if agencies too rapidly adopt intervention through natural networks without seriously considering the impact that sudden and heavy intervention would have on any natural system. Social systems, like physical ecological systems, are in delicate balance. Once upset, this balance may be slow to reestablish or may be permanently destroyed. Hasty or ill-considered professional intervention that is focused on only one aspect of a natural network may dislodge the central figure, who may then be permanently lost as an indispensable ally who is trying to improve the quality of life for the members of the network. The best safeguard, we believe, against inadvertent but nevertheless irreversible damage to natural systems is to introduce a practice widely recommended for physical systems—that is, to make an ecological impact study before initiating or collaborating on a project. Such a study will serve to counteract precipitate action and will offer an opportunity to view possible consequences from all angles.

We have stressed in earlier chapters and would like to stress again how important it is to prepare painstakingly the entry process and how necessary careful reconnaissance is prior to any intervention. It is exciting to speculate about the possible avenues of study and practice that may be opened up by introducing a new resource—natural networks—into the system of delivering social services. A look at the role natural networks may play could stimulate social workers individually and collectively to review their own history, to explore what other social sciences have contributed to social work theory and practice, and to analyze their own professional attitudes and methods as they join forces with natural neighbors in a new approach to an old ally.